FLYING WITH BOTH WINGS

Inventing the Past to Teach the Future

By
NEIL BREWER

PHI DELTA KAPPA
EDUCATIONAL FOUNDATION
Bloomington, Indiana
U.S.A.

Cover design by Victoria Voelker

Library of Congress Catalog Card Number 2001098915
ISBN 0-87367-837-0
Copyright © 2001 by Neil Brewer
Bloomington, Indiana U.S.A.

For Vicki, Jennifer, and Allison.
Love to you always, and many, many thanks.
Were it not for your love and enduring patience,
I am quite certain the old traveler
would simply have stayed home.

TABLE OF CONTENTS

INTRODUCTION

This is a story about many people. Most of them are real, some are not. A few are somewhere in between.

The real people in this story are the thousands of students who have taken the journey with Harmon Bidwell. Also very real are the scores of teachers, the hundreds of special assistants, and the dozens of community businesses and corporations who have supported Bidwell's annual adventure.

There are only a few characters who might not be considered real, yet they are undoubtedly among my favorites. And those who fall "somewhere in between" have become the most intriguing of all, particularly to children, whatever their age.

I believe it is safe to say that my imagination ran wild in the spring of 1993. The result was an epic journey called Harmon's Letters, and it has been the thrill of a very long lifetime. In fact, had I realized just how successful Harmon Bidwell would become, I would have neatly arranged for him to live at least another 10 to 15 years. But, as it is, this widely traveled character will most likely meet his end sometime sooner.

It's really only natural. Once we pass our 100th year, things begin to slow a bit; and Harmon reached that milestone back in 1998. This means that Harmon is himself close to that time of "becoming history." After all, he has left behind not only a delightful romp through the entire 20th century, but also has enlightened and enriched the lives of students at virtually every grade level along the way.

This is Harmon's story. But it also is my story. For this character, who is heavily wrinkled with age, who sweeps from the sky in his biplane to greet excited young learners, is the same person who teaches students in my classroom.

This book is partly about how I created and portray the traveler Harmon Bidwell. But it is much more. It is an attempt to encourage teachers to dream, to unleash the adventurer within themselves, and to immerse children in unending enrichment.

CHAPTER 1

FROM OUT OF THE BLUE

It began on the last day of school in June 1993.

About 1,000 kids from the elementary and next-door junior/ senior high school had just boarded the buses. As is the custom, every teacher — from kindergarten to the senior level — stood in two long columns to wave good-bye to the students for the summer. The bright-yellow buses rolled by slowly with a whole community's worth of kids packed inside. Scores of faces pressed against windows. Many were visibly happy, a few visibly sad, a few others a bit stunned, and some outright ecstatic.

Ironically, the faces of the teachers always reflect the same range of emotion — with most of them falling somewhere between the happy and ecstatic. My own feelings as the buses pulled out that day were what I would consider usual: a sudden realization that another year was gone, followed by great relief, then a strange and quiet emptiness on returning to my room.

As I often do when alone, I picked up my guitar and played a number of tunes. Nothing masterful — just the general chords necessary to enjoy a little Jàmes Taylor, Cat Stevens, or Paul McCartney. Sheer personal enjoyment. The kind that feels that way only when you take your time and concentrate on whatever it is you like to do.

I had seen great enjoyment spring from my students during that year. At least, I had seen it a few times. Certainly not often enough, but it had been there. And as I sat and strummed a bit more, those specific times began to come back to me.

Hadn't they loved making a video of something? Yes, but I had no recollection of what it was about. Let's see, what else? Ah, yes, our rockets! Not one student failed to build and launch a rocket. Good project. Anything else? Of course — camp! Those three days at the forestry were something they'll not forget. But what were some of the things they liked about it? Well, missing three days of regular school was nice. But I remember they said that singing at the campfires was one of the main things — and finding and opening a real owl pellet was just about the neatest thing ever!

Lots of great experiences, but everything in a jumbled heap.

I'm a classically jumbled heap of a teacher. A lot of us are. We have to be that way, at least some of the time, in order to keep so many different personalities headed in the same general direction. But who says we all have to go the same direction? Who would even want to? I know I wouldn't.

I thought about what projects the kids greatly enjoyed. I thought not only about the past year in my class, but about all the years, even back to when I was in school and about what have I seen being devoured by kids in other teachers' classrooms. Just a few minutes thinking about that many great projects resulted in a huge list, which put me right back to where I was, with a huge mix of unrelated stuff. But at that moment, an idea suddenly surfaced. What if a single character were somehow to experience each of the things that had been "unrelated" but successful in class? And even better, could such a character bring renewed life to those subjects or particular topics that had not enjoyed so much attention (or retention) by students?

I stopped strumming, for I was literally staggered by the idea. It overwhelmed me with a rush of thoughts that made me laugh out loud, and I started grabbing anything nearby on which I could scribble.

At first this project seemed to be so complicated and huge that there would be no way for it to ever become a reality. However,

Jerry Cook (left) interviews Harmon and hot-air ballonist Dan Silverman (Irvin Goldstein) at the first celebration and talent fair.

at that precise moment, the "way" walked in the door. Her name was Linda Ray; and though she was by no means the only person who would assist in the creation of Harmon's epic journey, I always will remember her clearly as the first who did so.

For years, all the teachers knew Linda as our "art à la carte" teacher supreme. On that fateful day, she was walking by my open door at the moment I was dwelling on Harmon's first adventure. I shouted at her, waving her toward me as she passed. Without me so much as even offering the pleasantry of a proper greeting, I launched into my story as soon as she came in the room.

For a full 10 minutes, Linda sat quietly and listened to me rant and rave in animated zeal until I felt I had released from within the main portion of what Harmon Bidwell could be all about. My excitement was uncontainable. I recall standing up, walking around, and sitting down again as the story burst forth.

"Hey! He could go this way and meet a scientist. . . . Which one? I don't care. I'll figure that out later. And if he turned left at this point in the state . . . no, no, let's make him turn right at this place because then he'd pass right by that historic landmark where they. . . ."

When I finished, I plopped back into my chair. Without the slightest hint of hesitation, Linda calmly said, "You have to do that."

Outright acceptance wasn't exactly what I had expected.

After all, I was talking about something that could be very expensive to pull off. I had no real dollar amount in mind; but Linda said she would do her best to come up with a thousand or so, provided, of course, that I write the thing up.

To me, this was a loudly ringing bell. The race gates had been opened, and Harmon was off! Possible funding had given me something to think about, but what stuck in my mind more than anything else from that first telling of the story was that I had been encouraged.

"You have to do that!"

It was a five-word sentence that would bring about tens of thousands of words over the following eight years — the words of this book included!

Actually, I'm not at all sure that hearing those words on that one occasion would have been enough for me to believe my idea was workable, or even sensible. But the fact that the next two people with whom I shared the story said exactly the same thing pretty well assured me that something was up.

On the other hand, it makes me think

Junior high school students hawk 5¢ Coca-Colas to eager fair-goers.

about how often our ideas fall onto the wrong ears. Had Harmon been shunned from the beginning, who knows what would have happened? Would I have felt the idea worthy enough to share again? Now, from the overwhelming evidence of the old traveler's success, I know I'll never let any idea be killed by negative first reactions. But back then? I can only be thankful that I was encouraged from the start to give it a try. These days, I know there are thousands of kids out there who are glad that I did; but in particular, I know of a homeroom class of students who have a special appreciation each year for the fact that their own teacher created something that they not only learn from, but also greatly enjoy.

For those of you who have created curricula for your own students, you know the immense satisfaction granted by such an effort. And for those of you who haven't, it is my contention there are only two basic reasons for you not having done so: 1) You have not received the correct dose of properly timed encouragement, or 2) You have yet to discover the fantastic learning experiences, for both you and your students, that always have been at your fingertips.

But fear not! The sole purpose of this book is to assist you in that discovery.

CHAPTER 2

THE TALE UNFOLDS

Time to sit and make yourself comfortable. I am going to tell you a story.

Harmon Bidwell was born in 1898 in Indianapolis, Indiana. His father's name was Edward, and his mother's name was Millie. Edward Bidwell was a successful crop inspector for the Indiana Department of Agriculture; and as a result, the Bidwells lived comfortably.

This condition of comfort was not taken for granted by Edward. He and his sister, Victoria Bidwell, had gone through very difficult times growing up in southern Indiana. Victoria was his caring, older sister and watched over him after their mother's death by the consumption in the mid-1850s. When their father, Jonathan, was taken into the Union Army, it was Victoria who saw as best she could to Edward's well-being when they were both placed in an overcrowded orphanage.

Upon their father's release from service, the three of them settled into farm life outside the small town of Lanesville; and it was there that Edward's interests in growing things developed. That led to his job in Indianapolis and to his eventual marriage to Millie. Victoria and her father had planned on making it to the wedding. But shortly before the day arrived, Jonathan Bidwell died.

Jonathan Bidwell lived nearly long enough to see his one and only grandchild, for less than a year later, Millie gave birth to Harmon.

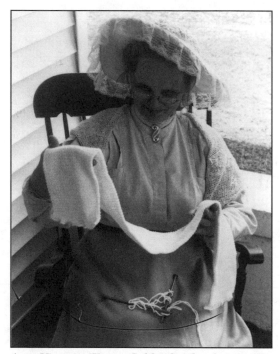

Aunt Victoria (Karen Cable) finishes knitting the scarf she will present to Harmon as a going-away present.

For the first eight years of his life, Harmon was surrounded by fine furnishings and plenty of friends in his well-to-do neighborhood. But in 1906, great sorrow befell the Bidwell home. His father had taken his mother along on one of his many railway business trips, leaving Harmon at the home of a friend. The cause for the collapse of the Franklin Bridge was never discovered; but when it did fall, seven were killed — two of the seven being Edward and Millie Bidwell. That tragedy marked the end of life in Indianapolis for Harmon and the beginning of his new one with his Aunt Victoria on the farm in Lanesville.

Life in Lanesville was slow, and often the work was very hard. But Harmon grew to love living in a small town. In the summers during his high school years, he worked for an old junk dealer named Lee Willard. It was during this time that he fixed up a rusted old Harley Davidson motorcycle that the old man had given him as payment for odd jobs. He became very attached to this somewhat faithful machine and eventually named it "Sir Davi," which he pronounced Sir Dah-vee.

In school, Harmon had studied to become a teacher. But first he wanted to see as much of the country as he could; so after final repairs were made on his motorcycle, he left home in June 1916 for what he thought would be a single summer of adventure. As it turned out, what happened on that journey forever changed his life.

He had promised his Aunt Victoria that he would write at least once a month and share everything that was happening on his adventure. And he did write, in tremendous detail. In many ways, he was a kind of teacher.

Aunt Victoria received Harmon's first letter in July 1916; and in its 43 pages, Harmon shares with her an amazing assortment of happenings. Of course, one of the first things he did was apologize for being so forgetful — for he left his new roadmap on the kitchen table. "Oh well," he writes, "I'll get another one . . . and I'll let you know in my letters which towns I pass through so you can follow my route!"

And this, his aged aunt happily did.

The first letter includes a meeting with a 10-year-old who gives Harmon a 1911 Christy Mathewson baseball card; the singing of the original "Take Me Out To The Ball Game"; the delicious discovery of Aunt Victoria's homemade oatmeal cookies hidden in his knapsack; a look at the first Indianapolis 500; the agony of motorcycle-riding muscle cramps, with the resulting creation of "The Rider's Workout"; and the unusual manner in which Harmon uses Sir Davi to help an old farmer fix a towering, long-rusted windmill.

This is only a sample of the many things he mentions in Letter #1; and by the time his aunt receives his eighth and final letter in February of 1917, the list of people and things he has somehow been involved with number in the hundreds!

Letter #8 reveals to Aunt Victoria a bit of a shock, because in it Harmon tells her that he won't be coming home. He has "simply seen too much of this glorious country and its wonderful people to allow it to be taken by the enemy," and he signed up for the French Air Service. "Sir Davi will be stored in a government warehouse until my return," he explains. And with a few parting words, his travels in the United States are evidently over.

Even though the battle stories coming out of Europe have inspired many young men to join in the war effort, Victoria Bidwell well knows about the realities of war. She now believes she will never see her nephew again.

For this reason, she decides to make Harmon the "teacher he always wanted to be, but never became." All she has to do, she reasons, is get Harmon's letters into the hands of teachers who would be willing to read his adventures in the classroom. Of course, she would add "a few" lessons on the side that might help bring out "this and that." She even would throw in some unique supplies here and there. But the main thing would be the letters themselves — a story to be shared with students by as many interested and inspiring teachers as she could find.

This premise was the original foundation of the Harmon's Letters program. Here she was, an elderly lady in 1917 who wanted to share her nephew's travels with students. And that's exactly what happened! With no real "time travel" explanation given to students, the teachers who first participated in Harmon's Letters in 1993 started the adventure with their kids by simply playing an introductory video. It was a film that was supposedly given them by Aunt Victoria herself, but she wasn't the "host" who appeared on the screen. (My gosh, no! You wouldn't catch her standing in front of any fancy motion picture machine!) No, that job was left to old Mr. Willard (expertly portrayed by my good friend, Lee Cable).

As a personal favor to the town's well-loved Victoria Bidwell, he explained to students all about Sir Davi, Harmon's travels, the letters, and Aunt Victoria's desire to now make Harmon the teacher he never became.

Keep in mind that this apparently was coming to the classroom straight from 1917! But things were about to get more time warped than that. Far more.

One of Aunt Victoria's inquiries that teachers would give out at the conclusion of a letter was the letter's 'puzzle.' She explained its vital importance to the class in a brief note:

Dear Students,

I hope that you enjoyed Harmon's first letter, and now I have something extra special to share with you.

Although many things happened to him in each letter, and he was always moving from place to place, he still managed to stay in at least one person's home long enough to get his letter completed and mailed from that spot. I've taken the return addresses from those places and hidden them within puzzles like this one. Therefore, once you've solved it, you'll know the precise place Harmon stayed! (And I know that if you will just write to those people, they're bound to write back with even more things to share about Harmon's visit with them!)

Sincerely,
Victoria Bidwell

Here's the puzzle for Letter #1:

Circles 1, 2, and 3: Add 110 to Harmon's "average speed" and you'll know what goes in these circles.

Circle 4: Harmon's motorcycle. ○○○ ○○○○

Circle 5: The Lincoln ○○○○○ is a good road.

Circle 6:- I'm so scared of heights, I'd never climb old ○○○○○○○ .

Circle 7: Sir Davi is really a ○○○○○○ ○○○○○○○○ motorcycle.

Circle 8: Something the Gray's prayed for. ○○○○

Circle 9: The Gray's live near ○○○○○ ○○○○○○○ .

Circle 10: Something Harmon sort of scribbles. ○○○

Circle 11: A terrible dry spell. ○○○○○○○

Teacher's Key for Puzzle #1

1, 2, and 3: Harmon's "average speed" is calculated by using the information in paragraphs two and three on page 4 of the letter. You may want to read it to them again or tell them that after riding for 4 hours, he reached a point 140 miles from home.

Answer: 140/4 = 35 mph. 110 + average speed = 145

4: Sir Davi
5: Trail

6: Maxwell
7: Harley Davidson
8: rain
9: Upper Sandusky
10: art
11: drought

Solution: 145 s t m a r k r d (St. Mark Rd.)

Complete Address: 145 St. Mark Rd.
Upper Sandusky, Ohio

As you can see, the solution at the bottom revealed a partial address. The teacher's manual supplied the key, and the remaining lines of the address were placed on the board after work on the puzzle had started. Soon, students had all the information they needed to venture directly into the past.

In the first year of the project, students from 11 schools wrote letters filled with questions about Harmon, Sir Davi, and their current whereabouts. I've hung on to hundreds of those letters, and most of them are well-composed examples from kids ranging from average to high achievement levels. Here are a few, brief letters from students who, their teachers later explained to me, were children who either had a very difficult time completing writing assignments or had very little interest in school. I have changed the students' names for these samples.

Dear Mrs Leffler,

I am Jessica Miller and I just wont to ask you a copul questions if you dont minid ok. I love when Mrs Amy reads harmons letter to us.

Do you still make duck calls and still set on your porch and make those calls. I would like to here that some time.

Have you ever seen Harmon after he took the quilt to the museum, and if you see hem a gein tell hem hi for me.

Thank you taking the time to read thes letter

Thank you
Your friend,
Jessica Miller

Dear Mrs. Lefler,

Hi my name is Chris Barrett I am 11 years old I have a honda motar bike.

Does Mr. Kelams ever come by in the morning?

Do you ever cook meals realy big? Do you ever shop at the barney Krogers? Have you seen another motar bike since sir davi?

Sincerly

Chris Barrett

These letters are among my favorites because they show a real effort being made by kids who want to share something of themselves with the characters of Harmon's journey.

To this day, one of the most rewarding parts of the entire adventure is the student responses. But it wasn't without its snags in the first few years of the program. After all, students were communicating with persons across seven or eight decades!

After the students had solved the puzzle and had an address, getting them to write return letters was no problem. Granted, some of the letters from students were big collections of questions, but that still meant they'd listened to the letter that had been read to them. And for the most part, those kids turned out letters that were filled with understanding and even compassion for a character they'd never met! ("He didn't really start smoking after seeing that sign, did he? I hope not, because my uncle . . .")

While Harmon's Letters were enjoyed by students of every intellectual level, I still wanted the journey to be as realistic as possible, even for those who did not believe that they could be swept into the possibility that it was real. However, I suspected that the classic 11- or 12-year-old wanted to hang onto the fantastic as long as possible; and when those return letters from 1917 found their way to the teachers' desks, the fantastic became reality.

Here's how it worked:

Students from the 11 schools solved the puzzle and wrote letters. The teachers then put the letters into one large envelope and "mailed" them. This might mean a student would be selected with a great deal of ceremony to take the envelope to the office for the secretary to put in the out-going mail. The teachers would pick them up later and take them home. I showed up on their doorstep later that night to get the letters.

I'd read through the letters as quickly as possible and wrote one return letter for each class, targeting some of the kids' specific questions for personal answers. At first, this was a task I completed alone. But with letters from hundreds of students, the job soon became overwhelming. Fortunately, several interested teachers volunteered to help, and the return writing was enjoyable as we read and discussed the piles of inquisitive, and often touching letters students had sent to whichever character had been revealed to them through the puzzles.

One of the first things teachers presented in the classroom was "The Art of Beautiful Writing" inquiry. I had been able to obtain hundreds of calligraphy pens at a discount. Thus scores of excited kids could compose their messages with their own calligraphy pens, and our return letters were written the same way. But the envelopes were the real clincher.

I made the envelopes out of thick, brown paper, similar to butcher paper. I had a huge roll of it left from some stained glass projects; and after carefully cutting out and folding one master envelope, I simply unfolded it and used it as a template for the dozens that would follow. The appearance of these large, antiquated envelopes was strange enough, but they were finished with a pair of time-warped oddities that would have many a student making more than one double take at what had arrived. These were, of course, the proper stamps used in 1917 and the correctly matching postmarks. Finding actual, uncirculated 2 cent stamps from that time period turned out to be easy. The first stamp and coin shop I went to had them; and after explaining what I'd be using them for, the dealer sold them to me for half off.

The postmark was a much more difficult task. It appeared that the only way I could get realistic, properly dated cancellations on the stamped envelopes was to have rubber stamps made for the job. This time, there was no discount. The seven rubber stamps that were required cost $110. I still recall the hesitation I had in paying for the rubber stamps in order to add such an apparently small detail in the program. However, if you look at the photo of the result, I think you'll agree that it was worth it.

Teachers often told me about their students' delight when the class received one of those huge return envelopes filled with responses to their queries about someone, or something, that somehow was happening both at that moment and 80 years ago.

Weird, huh? Of course it was! But all the while, kids from all over southern Indiana were deeply engaged in the accompanying activities surrounding this unknown entity called Harmon. Windmills of every imaginable size and shape had been built, class quilts had been sewn, radio shows had been recorded, silent films had been produced, and women's rights were upheld enthusiastically. By the middle of May, Harmon's trek of decades past seemed to have been successful in every way possible. The journey was about to end along with the school year.

Ahhh, but Aunt Victoria had one more surprise up the sleeve of her laced-covered dress!

Near the end of the year, each participating class received an unusual bit of communication. They were telegrams — from 1917, no less — and they led the way to an amazing finale: Harmon was returning, and I would be him.

That first year, we decided that we would bring all 11 classes together at a beautiful, privately owned farm. Because I believed that it would be the only time that the program would conclude in such a way, I went for broke. I decided to have a real barbershop quartet to sing at some point in the show, an actual hot air balloon on the scene, and a professional photographer to get the best possible shots of the class groups. I also decided that I simply could not do without obtaining the spitting image of Harmon's motorcycle to carry me up and over the hill at just the right moment.

And, as if this was not enough, there was a real biplane that would land at its precisely scheduled time to pick up Harmon and carry him off to Texas, leaving Sir Davi behind to be tended by a trusted old friend, Mr. Lee Willard himself.

Whew! It still rattles my brain at times to think of how that all came together, and all those elements were only the "big chunks" of the puzzle! The smaller pieces numbered in the dozens. Hand-dipped ice cream, 8-oz glass-bottled Coca-Colas, and Hershey's bars went for a nickel each. Classes made quilts and windmills, and these were displayed by the kids. Homemade rockets were fired, and an antique truck was proudly shown by its owner. Of course, the talent fair was in progress from the moment the first bus arrived, emceed by none other than Mr. Willard.

Students cooperated and stayed within the half-acre that was roped off for the event. Student acts appeared on the stage throughout the morning, intermingled with the arranged "professional" acts. As you would no doubt assume, the acts by the students far and away made for the more memorable moments, particularly those bits that were created to be 'live commercials' for the community sponsors of the fair.

The day was one I'll never forget, for several reasons. First, the weather was perfect. Not just very good, but absolutely pristine. Low humidity, slight breeze, and blue, blue skies. Ideal for the kids, teachers, and parents who were seated on hay bales in the sun and picture perfect for the biplane pilot to fly to the farm and land on the grass airstrip without problems. (Yes, this particular farm has its own runway.)

Second, I was overwhelmed with the satisfaction that the whole thing had actually come together and was now coming to life, right in front of me. This made me laugh aloud at one point, as I saw everything unfolding in its prepared order from my hiding place in the nearby woods. I watched all from afar through binoculars, sitting astride the 1920 Harley Davidson loaned to me for the occasion. My cue to appear — Lee Willard leaning back with a long drink from a Coke bottle — would come late in the program. After all, suspense needed to be built around the fact that this Harmon character may not show, that he might not, in fact, even exist!

He existed, all right. He was dressed in rented World War One riding gear atop his faithful motorcycle with his talent fair agenda in hand, waiting for his assigned moment. The barbershop quartet had just finished, and Aunt Victoria had been invited onto the hay wagon stage. She slowly made her way up the steps, as the sound of a far off biplane was heard. I couldn't believe it. It had been due to arrive a little earlier, and I'd thought for a while that the plane wasn't coming for some unknown reason. But there it was! These kids were about to see two more vintage machines, and one would carry me off into the blue before their wondering eyes.

Although the owner of the Harley desperately tried, he was unable to get his prized cycle to start the day before. I was looking forward to actually riding it across the field between my location and the students; but at that moment, it seemed even better to have to struggle with pushing the heavy thing. The students well knew of Harmon's common misfortune with Sir Davi from his letters, and to have to admit he had carelessly run out of gas fit his persona perfectly!

Needless to say, it was an unbelievable feeling to suddenly appear from the woods and have hundreds of kids staring in amazement as I made my way across the field. Harmon would have been 19 years old in May of 1917. I was 37, but that was an age completely concealed by my riding attire, which included floppy hat, huge goggles, and just the right touch of facial roadway mud. Not 24 hours earlier in the classroom, I had sported a thick, bristly mustache. Now, it was gone, and it was uncanny how many years had disappeared with it. With my mustache missing and me wearing my costume, I was unrecognizable even to my own sixth-grade students! Early in the day I had called in "sick" and was then patched into my room's speaker-phone to tell my kids how terribly sorry I was because I wouldn't be able to make it to school and that the principal would be taking them to the fair in my place.

"Have a good time without me," I told them. Ha! Without me? No way!

I may have written this adventure to motivate kids, but I was not about to leave myself out! And now, here I was, in front of my own class, as well as hundreds of other unknown students all around me. They reached out with crumpled Hershey's wrappers for me to autograph. I was called to the stage; and as I dismounted "Sir Davi," a girl in my class was standing close by. It was time to let an inside secret out, so I quietly said, "Hi, Stephanie!" as I walked by. Looking through those mud-splattered goggles as her mouth fell open was something I'll always remember.

I could see the word spreading fast that Mr. Brewer was Harmon, and I had a premonition of disaster. But it quickly became evident that the "home" kids were proudly containing their secret as best they could.

It was a great day, even though the biplane pilot didn't land and later claimed that he never saw any of the 14 bright yellow school buses parked in a row alongside the open field below. That part was frustrating, but it has since become a long-running joke that I was better off not boarding a plane with a pilot who could miss such a beacon.

Harmon eventually made a somewhat less exciting exit via the same manner in which he had arrived. But the overall success of his travels in the classroom had been huge, and this first year's talent fair had been an ideal culminating event. However, what was to come was even better. For the next two years, more and more teachers joined the original 11, bringing the total to 20; and dozens of new inquiries were added to the manual. The weather for the second and third years was again perfect, and each time an open cockpit biplane did land, making my exit a thrill not only for the kids, but one for me as well. In fact, the pilot enjoyed his part so much that he informed me that he'd make his plane available for the Harmon's Letters program anytime it was possible for him to do so!

There were many elements that made these annual gatherings unforgettable. But one memorable (and sometimes nagging) reason was that it was all a bit too surreal, almost to the point of being within the Twilight Zone. After all, here was a large group of kids who had been convincingly introduced to Harmon by a film with Lee Willard as its host. Yet, supposedly, Lee Willard was a middle-aged junk dealer in 1917! And a telegram to the class from Harmon's Aunt Victoria? My gosh . . . she was born in 1850!

No, enough was enough. If Harmon's adventure was to somehow continue in such a realistic format, it was time to figure out a way to have him become a part of the present.

The idea for Harmon's 'new' life came about as quickly as his original existence had, but with a lot of questions and answers to myself about the possible problems:

Aviator Robert Herbstreit helps unstrap Harmon while a young interviewer prepares to broadcast Harmon's first words to the waiting crowd at Cedar Farm.

"Let's see . . . How old would Harmon be today, if I kept all of the "time line factors" the same?"

"Why bother?"

"Why Bother?! I'll tell you 'why bother'. . . because this thing has been a ton of work and because all of the activities that have been created (as well as the letters themselves) were written to go along with an adventure that took place beginning in 1916!"

"Oh."

"So like I said, how old would he be?"

"Well, this is 1995. Everything was centered on a character who was born in 1898 . . . So, if he was born in June . . . That makes him 97 years old this coming June!"

"Perfect!"

And so the quest to bring Harmon completely into the present was under way. The introductory film that would introduce him to students would have to be changed. Aunt Victoria's comments about student inquiries would be removed. And, of course, the biggest change of all would be made to the character of Harmon himself.

It occurred to me that it would be interesting to have a grandson of Harmon's find his letters. This young relative would then have the same desire his great-great aunt had, only now it was to make "Grandfather Harmon" the teacher he wanted to be but never became. A new introductory film was made with the kind assistance of a former student of mine, Seth Willis; and it still is used as the beginning of Harmon's journey in classrooms all over the state.

Quite simply, it is a six-minute hook that latches onto hundreds of new travelers every year and carries them away to the thematic adventure of a lifetime.

A lifetime? Definitely. For with the character of Harmon still alive, he has now been through an entire century of adventure, not a mere eight letters' worth! And Seth eventually shares with the students those things that happened after the letters — namely, his grandfather's book-length tale from France as a World War One pilot and his return to the United States to fly as a freelance newspaper reporter. (Thus the natural appearance of Harmon in his biplane, the same one he used in France!)

Considering the time spent on creating the original teacher's manual, changing the notes from Aunt Victoria was no problem. I simply made them all appear to have been written by Seth. (I liked the sound of Seth Bidwell, so we kept Seth's real first name.) As for the existence of a 97-year-old Harmon, that was another matter. It would be expensive, to say the least, to have a professional make-up artist convert me to a soul comparable in appearance to Dustin Hoffman's 120-year-old Little Big Man, but that was precisely the task at hand.

Harmon was transferred to the present successfully, and he continues to appear annually at student talent fairs in several locations throughout Indiana. Where it isn't possible to land in a biplane, he drives to the scene on an immaculate 1950 Harley Davidson.

The expenses of such an endeavor would certainly appear overwhelming; and at times, I admit, I was not sure where the required funds would come from. But they came, and they continue to arrive. However, it should be duly noted that 'required funds' are quite often more accurately described as 'required friends.' And with such friends, I have been abundantly blessed.

CHAPTER 3

A FITTING EXAMPLE

Harmon's adventure, though elaborate, is only an example of the way teachers can create a curriculum incorporating any topic.

Because a character such as Harmon can travel almost anywhere, almost anything can be written into the program. For example, in the first letter I wanted students to appreciate elders, sing, think hard before smoking, consider the safety of wearing a helmet, learn calligraphy, bake oatmeal cookies, eat them, exercise, do some baseball math, and learn a little bit about the conservation of energy through the construction of various windmills. All were worthy topics. But just as important, I wanted students to simply enjoy the journey.

That first letter covered the above academic topics, as well as many more. And the enjoyment — for both students and myself — seemed to spring forth as a natural byproduct of the curriculum. The agenda was packed. Although I knew there could always be additions, I was satisfied with the lineup for the moment. However, that moment quickly passed.

Mike Kaiser, a sixth-grade teacher and one of the original 11 teachers who piloted Harmon, asked me to include a favorite activity his students enjoyed every year. Mike gives his kids 25 "fast-food size" drinking straws and a certain amount of Scotch tape. The students then construct a protective device that will hold a raw egg and, they hope, save it from breaking when it is dropped from the roof of the building to the playground (a task reserved for the school's custodian).

Mike's egg-drop inquiry was the first outside suggestion I added to Harmon's trek. It was easy to incorporate the activity into the first letter. It became just one more activity on a huge "pick and choose" list for investigation by students.

In Letter #1, Harmon finds himself high on top of a rusted windmill (named Maxwell) in Ohio, trying to get it working again for an old farmer who can no longer climb the tower. The connection to Mike's egg-drop activity was simple. All I had to do was go back into my computer and add a few new paragraphs.

> *He had already pulled the long brake handle that led to the top of the mill; and looking straight up, I could see that the old brake was still able to do its job. Even with a fairly strong gust of wind now and then, the big blades were locked up tight.*
>
> *I tied the chain on with the rope just as he had done, and climbed to the top without stopping. When I was once again standing on the tower's platform, I loosened the chain from the rope and started to haul it upward. Far below, Mr. Gray kept it from tangling up on the ground and was shouting instructions up to me to either "Slow down!" or "Go on with it!"*
>
> *I think he enjoyed the part of the foreman on the job, and I liked the part of the laborer as well. When it looked like I had reached about the halfway point on the chain, I pulled up a few more feet and then hooked it over the gear.*
>
> *When I was up there before, I hadn't noticed a small bird's nest that was neatly wedged in a knothole in one of the almost rotted through floorboards, and I didn't see it this time either until I had stepped on the end of the board.*
>
> *The resulting shaking of the old wood caused the nest to suddenly fall through the hole, and I felt a sinking in my chest as I caught a dashing glimpse of a single light-blue egg caught in the twines of the nest as it plummeted toward certain destruction.*
>
> *I watched as it spiraled through the center of Max's iron girders and was amazed at the luck of it not hitting any of them on*

its way to the bottom. It was a long, agonizing trip; but when it did finally meet the earth, I waited for Mr. Gray to shout up the bad news. He had watched it too, and we had both fallen silent from our work at the onset of this unfortunate event.

The nest landed on the concrete base of the well's pump — making me expect the worst — so you can imagine my complete surprise when Mr. Gray took a step toward it, leaned over to inspect the damage, and then nearly fell over backward as he looked straight up to me and hollered, "Didn't even scratch it!"

Some things are surely wonders of nature . . . and others are complete luck . . . and on that day, I think I'd witnessed both at the same time! Mr. Gray shouted that we'd put it back later, and he carefully gathered the nest in both hands and carried it over to a shady spot by the barn. As I climbed back down, Mr. Gray was already back to the task at hand by busily hammering the two long ends of the chain together with a master link. While he did that, I walked over by the barn to see what else could be done to get Sir Davi ready.

There by the wall sat the nest, and I took a moment to kneel down and again marvel at what had happened. Shadows of the giant windmill were cast in dark long x's across the barn; and looking back and up at the tremendously high platform, I figured that egg must have fallen a distance at least a thousand times its own height. The nest had surely helped, but it was a mere straggling of loosely bound dried grass and twigs that probably weighed less than the egg itself.

I pulled a few nearby weeds and lightly covered it, thinking I could take it back to the top later, but for now — back to work.

As you can see, it only took a brief insertion to include the premise for Mike to set aside Harmon's first letter and say, "Well! This is certainly a good stopping point because we have a special inquiry that fits in perfectly with Harmon's episode with the bird's nest!"

You might be quick to say, "Fine. Nice egg-drop thing. How clever to add it to a letter with a windmill in it. But what about the topics students study at my school? In health we study the

heart, in science we do the earthquake stuff, and in language arts
we work on sentence structure and poetry." But the beauty of
designing curricula within a story such as Harmon's is that the
creative possibilities are endless.

The heart? Why couldn't he have been born with a hole in his
own? Or at least a slight murmur. No doubt Aunt Victoria would
be terrified at the thought of some of the things her nephew might
subject himself to along the way that could trigger a problem, and
he would be constantly reassuring her in his writings that he was
doing all the right things that Doctor Whoever had told him to do
to maintain his health.

When it was time to make the tough climb up the high ladder
of the windmill, students would be on the edge of their seats wondering if it was something he should be attempting.

What about classroom inquiries to accompany such a thing? Just
as endless. Students could climb steps to match Harmon's climb
and check pulse rates and blood pressure. If the letter revealed
Harmon's weight and the limits where his own pulse and pressure
were supposed to remain, you might even have someone of similar
weight do the climb as the class watched. They would be concerned
about Harmon if the readings surpassed Harmon's limitations.

And what about this? Your students may have done some
"open heart surgery" in class with real hearts from various animals. It is a tremendous experience for kids, and we've opened a
few ourselves; but the connection to it doesn't currently exist in
any of Harmon's letters. But what if Harmon worked for a week
or so in a slaughterhouse? He's always having to make a little
traveling money by doing odd jobs here and there. Perhaps a portion of his letter to Aunt Victoria would read something like this:

*So I'm sorry if I've unintentionally changed your plans for
your next meal. But Aunt, I don't think I'll be eating a whole
lot more of it either until the memory of this particular job washes
cleanly away!*

*On another, and much more fascinating, matter, I was given
the task last evening to throw out all the beef innards that had*

been swept up in what they call the "Organ Master's" room. It's really a lot bigger than what you might call a room — more like a concrete barn, I'd say. But anyway, one large box I hauled to the dumpster out back was filled with cows' hearts, and I couldn't help but take a few extra moments to take one out of the box and take a good, close look. I know it may sound silly, but the first thing that shot through my mind was that this had been beating inside a healthy animal just a single day before! I didn't have a lot of time to waste, but I couldn't help running my fingers into one of the tubes. I don't know if it was a vein or an artery, but it was a big one, coming right out of the top of the heart and then branching off in two directions. Back in high school, I remember reading that the heart is the toughest muscle in the human body. Maybe that goes for cows, too! It was incredibly tough; and no matter how hard I tugged at the tubes or the outside surface, there was no way I could get any of it apart to see what might be inside.

A passage such as this would get kids excited about dissecting a heart. And while you might argue that students would be excited about the activity anyway, there is an elevated element of intrigue about an ongoing story that keeps students talking and thinking about widely varied aspects of the topic long after any particular piece of that topic was covered. Kids get attached to the main characters you create in thematic journeys, and they attempt to figure them out or out-guess them, causing many opportunities for deep, critical thinking.

You certainly noticed the opening lines about whatever it was that Harmon had seen going on in the slaughterhouse. His warnings to Aunt Victoria were genuine; meat-packing plants did have huge sanitation problems in those days. (Do any meat-packing plants still exist? Where?) And what about the animal rights consciousness that seems to strike him at the dumpster? (Is anybody in the room a vegetarian? Why?)

If I ever do put a segment like this in one of Harmon's letters (and I'm feeling the inspiration to do just that), I'm sure the reaction will be extremely vocal as it's being shared in the classroom. Students will be calling out correct parts of the heart (if we've reviewed them) as Harmon mentions the "pieces." And if the class hasn't yet studied the heart, what better place to put the letter down and begin such a pursuit?

Another example is an insertion that I did put into Harmon's seventh letter. A few years ago, a teacher who was listening to my presentation about Harmon raised a hand and asked if I had anything about AIDS in the story. I didn't, of course, because the virus surfaced in the early 1980s and might not have even existed before the 1950s. But, as always, when a comment comes up pertaining to teaching a particular topic through the story, I told the teacher that I was sure AIDS could be covered.

This caused me to dig into a few things about blood-related diseases. After no more than ten minutes of inquiry, I had what I needed. Apparently, there is a slew of diseases transferred by body fluids, and hepatitis has a long history. All I needed to do was to put Harmon into a situation where he is responsible for his own actions and connect it with students being made more aware of their own actions.

> *As I made my way out, the cook called out for me not to miss his boy's lemonade stand just up the road, and at once a picture from my own days of summertime salesmanship came clearly to mind. I called back with a wave that I wouldn't miss it, even if it was a 40-some-odd degree day. And when I stopped Sir Davi in front of the tiny establishment about 100 feet from the diner, I was pleased to see that the noble art of lemonade stand construction hadn't been lost. I'm sure you remember the assortment of stands I went through as a boy. Every summer brought on slightly new improvements over the previous year's design; and by far my greatest innovation was undoubtedly the roof, which I remember came along in the third summer, rightly following two years of bad sunburn.*
>
> *This boy wouldn't have any problem with that, though, because not only was his stand a classic piece of well-roofed archi-*

tecture, he also had an extreme advantage over any competitors by peddling his refreshments in the middle of the winter. His "Lemonade" sign spanning the distance above the counter brought back more memories. I myself had never been bold enough to ask for more than 3 cents a glass, but each end of this sign boldly advertised the full charge of a nickel.

No one seemed to be around; but when I turned my motor off, the familiar and distinctive rattling of a ladle in a pitcher came from behind the counter. And sure enough, when I leaned over the table for a peek, there sat the second reddest-headed person I'd ever seen stirring up a fresh batch. Even with a good-sized woolen hat covering most of it, the hair that stuck out down around his ears and eyebrows looked like a fully ripened pumpkin, and there was little doubt I'd found the cook's eight- or nine-year-old son.

He glanced up from his work and said, "I heard you pull in. I'm just opening up, and I'll be with you in a jiffy!" Then he handed me up two wooden signs and asked if I'd hang them up for him. One was the "Open" sign, and the other had a cut-out of an Indian glued to it. Beneath the old warrior's face, the boy had printed the words, " Chief Red Head — Great Leader of the Chair Key Tribe." I didn't think much of it until the boy suddenly popped up with the pitcher in hand and an Indian headdress on in place of his winter cap. I ordered up a glass and, while I searched my pockets for the change, told him that I thought the decorations added a nice selling point to his business. "Oh, it's no selling kind of thing," he said, "I just want to offer membership to anybody who stops by and wants to be a part, that's all."

As I laid down my nickel, I couldn't help but ask, "A part of what?"

"Just history," he said.

"History?"

"Sure! See my sign? That's Chief Red Head, great leader of the Chair Key Tribe, and I'm a direct descendent of his. You can be too if you wanna be."

I took a hard look at the picture of the Indian and then took an equally long sizing-up stare at the boy. His face and hands were as white and freckly as any pale-face there ever was, and I laughed a bit at the fun of it.

"How do I go about pulling that trick off?" I asked.

"There's no trick," he said. "All you need to do is be a blood brother, and you're in! See right here?"

He reached down behind the counter and pulled out a ragged notebook. On its cover were some hand-drawn pictures of a buffalo, and a bow and arrow that were supposed to, I was sure, resemble the kind you'd see painted on the side of a teepee. He turned the book in my direction and quickly flipped to pages full of the names of people that he said were once "regular old plain Americans" but were now recorded in his official Chair Key History Book as honorary changed-over blood brothers.

"What's this 3 cents and a check mark doing by everybody's name," I asked.

"Well, of course there's a small charge to be a member, but three cents is awful cheap when you figure that Indians would hunt for days and then pay for things with animal hides that they skinned down. And besides that, this is the only place you can get to be a real descendent like me."

Well, Aunt, it was all too good to pass up. Where else would I ever get an ice cold glass of lemonade in January and a place in history, all for less than the cost of a skinned-down squirrel?

I laid down another three cents; and while I signed the book, Little Chief Red Head disappeared behind the counter. When he came back up he had two smears of mud on his cheeks and a thorn bush limb in his hand. There wasn't any need to say anything, I just held out my hand, ready to take it like a brave. He stuck his own thumb first, then gave mine a jab. "Nisho Bocka Weecha," he said as he pushed our bleeding thumbs together, and my claim to a place with the Chair Keys was sealed.

As I climbed aboard Sir Davi, an auto pulled in and a little girl jumped out the back door. "Nisho Bocka Weecha!" was her call to the boy, and he returned the cry while he poured her *a glass. The girl's dad rolled his eyes at me with a smile; and as he walked by, he held up his own thorn-pricked thumb and said, "Did George get you, too?"*

"I'm a member," I said, and drove away.

This incident in the adventure leads directly to the discussion of Harmon's apparent lack of common sense and responsibility, but it's quickly brought out that he was most likely ignorant of any underlying possibilities. Students are reminded that they have all the evidence they need in today's world about AIDS — there simply isn't the option to say, "But I didn't know!" However, students continue to require constant reinforcement of the facts, so the teacher's manual includes an inquiry called Blood Brothers that vividly demonstrates the hazards of the exchange of body fluids.

Including topics such as this is vital, but the curriculum would be sorely lacking were it not for the life given it by the fine arts, along with those extra touches of fascination that seem to catch and hold onto everyone's attention.

One subject I include in this realm of the fascinating is rocketry. Every student I've ever had enjoys seeing their homemade creation lift skyward. And the areas of study in this particular field are many, with math and science being but an obvious two.

When Harmon meets soon-to-be rocket pioneer Robert Goddard, the scientist is still having great difficulties with even the shortest of successful flights with his new, liquid-powered invention. People all around Worcester, Massachusetts, have relentlessly taunted and jeered the man for years, dubbing him "The Mooney," a name attributed to Goddard's revealed desire to eventually build a rocket that could carry a man to the moon.

Harmon knows nothing of the subject, and his time spent with Goddard doesn't add all that much to his knowledge of rocketry. But, of course, it's a different matter for the students involved!

From the ancient Chinese to the Space Shuttle, the history of rocketry is covered in an opening overhead presentation; and when the real Dr. Robert Goddard goes up on the screen, kids light up with the "connection fascination" so familiar to activities associated with Harmon's journey. The song associated with his encounter with Goddard is "Shine on Harvest Moon," an old-time, barbershop quartet classic. Adding the song to the activities was especially satisfying for two reasons. It exposes kids to a type of music about which they have virtually no awareness, and it also stirs pleasant memories of another time in my own life, bedtime at home for my younger brother, Brian, and myself. Realizing now that it was a mere ploy to calm our rowdy selves down, my parents would play Reader's Digest records on the Magnavox. Beautiful melodies wafted from the living room into our own, and the hundreds of classics we learned by heart as we lay half awake planted themselves solidly in our minds. Forgive me for the opinion, but it really was great music! And a further opinion would be that I have always felt that my own students need more exposure to it. Kids captivated by a story will take on more variety than they may normally accept through general curricular doses.

Ahh, once again, the beauty of it all! Do I think Scott Joplin's "Alexander's Ragtime Band" deserves some attention? Absolutely.

The composer died in 1916 (the same year Harmon's travels began), making the timing perfect for easy insertion of his music nearly anywhere I wanted it. But this man's contribution would be placed in one of the most intriguing spots of all. As the original, piano-playing "entertainer," I feel certain that Joplin would be pleased to find his music being enjoyed by students who were simultaneously enthralled with another world-class act: Charles Chaplin.

But before I get on with how students actually see Harmon in a real Charlie Chaplin silent film, I have once again been suddenly sidetracked.

It just occurred to me that I could have written into a letter that Harmon had an extra fondness for ragtime music. If so, he could have gone to Scott Joplin's funeral and found himself among the great grandfathers of jazz. Perhaps you can name a few. I don't know of any from that early time period, but they would have shown up for a wake. Just think of the music they'd send Scott off with! For weeks thereafter, students would enjoy hearing you play his great instrumentals during their work times throughout the day. For some, it would undoubtedly be their "Magnavox." Many would gladly research Scott Joplin. They would discover his historic roots in slavery. Who knows? They may even add jazz to their personal top 40 — even if they'd never dream of confessing to it!

That's the magic of self-written curricula. The state standards teachers seek to appease don't have to be realized through the study of the general texts. All of these standards can be covered successfully while the children are enriched with your own connected concoction.

Although dozens of other examples of inserted fascination have made Harmon's letters the joy they have been, I suppose I'll limit myself to two more favorites, then move onward. The first of these favorites involves, as I said, Charlie Chaplin. The second involves the Beatles.

During the writing of the letters back in 1993, I knew that I wanted students to be involved somehow in making films; for in doing so, they can't help but be drawn into a world of output that I have yet to see matched by any other activity, hands down. The process of putting together a movie contains almost every life skill you can list; and it involves the extensive application of writing, editing, and oral presentation skills.

Third-grader David Brown puts on his best Charlie Chaplin smile.

For the insertion of film making into a letter, the timing of Harmon's journey could not have been better. I was familiar with the fact that Chaplin's biggest years were somewhere around 1916, but I had no idea of what I would discover one day while watching his film, *The Fireman*, with my brother, Brian.

The picture is silent, of course, and Charlie Chaplin is his usual, charming, bungling self. He has enlisted as a fireman; and after all sorts of mayhem, he finds himself at the reins of two huge and raging horses that are pulling his reeling fire wagon helter-skelter through the town and then down rugged back roads to reach a blazing farmhouse.

Just before he reaches the house, the wagon careens around a corner. In the road stands a man with a shovel. For what cinematic reason he is there, I have never been able to detect. He is simply in the middle of the dirt road, apparently filling up a few holes. He is seen twice in the film, for a total of maybe four seconds; but when I saw him for the first time that day with Brian, I couldn't help but shout out, "There he is! Look at that! Rewind that! Play it again! My gosh, it's Harmon!"

Little did I know, those same words were soon to be repeated again and again by thousands of students. To this day, I still get calls from teachers who say that their kids had them rewind that fleeting glimpse of Harmon over and over. The man in the road actually looks fairly generic for the time period — flat cap, white shirt, suspenders, long pants — but the fact that his back is turned at just the right angle to the camera (as Chaplin streaks by) makes for the perfect continuation of a mysterious soul whose face may never be seen.

The instant I saw "Harmon" standing there, I knew *The Fireman* had to be included in the program. It was just a matter of figuring out how to put the premise for showing it in the classroom into a letter home to Aunt Victoria. Here's how it was done, picking up with Harmon driving in New York City.

. . . anyway, I was slowly making my way in heavy traffic down Harper's Boulevard when I suddenly caught the sight of

thick black smoke drifting high over the street up ahead. It was coming from off to the right, and it looked as though the next turn off in that direction was at least a fourth of a mile away.

The traffic had slowed to a snail's pace, and all at once came to a complete halt. Heads came from behind steering wheels and out of windows all around to shout out their usual "Hey's!" and "What's goin' on up there?!"

I could plainly see what was going on, and I wasn't about to sit in stalled traffic yelling about it! A building was burning, and I had to help any way I could! What if the police or even an ambulance couldn't get through this mess? Everybody else may have been stuck where they were, but I certainly wasn't!

This was a spot for a man on a motorcycle, and I happened to be right on top of one. I pulled Sir Davi around the auto in front of me and sped by. There were six lanes of traffic, three in each direction, and I was the only driver doing any moving at all on the entire street. The smoke continued to billow in heavy clouds as I neared the street it was coming from; and when I reached the intersection, I couldn't help but yell at the drivers who had stopped their autos in front of all of us to watch the flames.

"You blasted sightseers!"

I noticed the sign said, "Jefferson Street"; and as I turned on to it and sped toward the blaze, I couldn't make out what a police officer that had been standing at the intersection shouted to me, but I was sure it was something like, "Hurry up! I've called for more help, but it hasn't arrived! You may be our only hope!"

With this encouragement I raced towards the 4- or 5-story building halfway down the block. Smoke poured from its second floor, and now I could clearly see flames shooting from its open windows. A large crowd of curious onlookers stood packed together about 100 feet from its front door, and no one appeared to be attempting any rescue! Not only that, as I sped toward the group, I saw a woman waving her arms out of the second story window, screaming like a siren!

This was too much! I would have to deal with the inhumanity of New Yorkers some other time! This woman had to be saved, and be saved now!

I brought my machine to a sliding sideways stop, hollered for the nearest man to hold it for me, and ran past the rest of the stunned crowd to reach the helpless victim. Two policemen appeared from nowhere and ran behind me, and I was glad to have their assistance. "Come on!" I yelled back to them, and kept running. The people of the crowd were now cheering wildly, and a blast of adrenaline pumped my legs even faster.

Just before I reached the front door, I took a quick glance to the window . . . and she was gone! Fast action was now a matter of life or death! I grabbed the knob, jerked the door open. . .

. . . and there she stood. She looked bewildered, mad, and I must say quite beautiful all at the same time.

"Who in the world are you?!" was all I remember her saying.

The words had no sooner left her lips when I felt the grip of the two police officers on both my arms, and a man from somewhere behind me screamed,

"cut!. . . CUT!. . . CUT!!!"

Between the laughter of the crowd, and the sound of total disgust in the man's voice, I didn't know what to think. The police still had me by the arms; and as they practically dragged me back across the street, the one on my right said, "Now you've done it!" and the other one added, "And the chief said this was the last day of this movie stuff on downtown streets too! It's been piling up traffic for weeks!"

As we approached the man who was obviously in charge, he hopped down off the large chair he was on. He was short, heavy, and he must have had some kind of eye problem because, even though the sky was cloudy, he was wearing darkened glasses.

The people who were jammed in behind wooden barricades a few feet back continued laughing and squeezed even tighter together to hear what he had to say when they saw him take a step toward me. Naturally, I thought we'd shake hands; and I'd apologize for whatever I had done, even if it was somehow wrong, to try and help the lady. He raised his hand; but instead of reaching for my out-stretched one, he pointed at me and said, "Officers, arrest this man! . . . and impound that infernal motorcycle along with him!"

My disbelief with what I was hearing was accented by the crowd becoming absolutely silent. They had had their fun with me, or at me, I should say, but they weren't laughing anymore. This man was in a rage, and he continued . . . "I have had it with these imbecilical interruptions! I demand you remove him at once!"

One of the officers mumbled that he didn't think it had come to this, and somebody booed from somewhere in the crowd. That prompted more booing, and a man shouted, "Aw, he didn't mean nothin' by it!" and before long, the whole group was chanting: "Let the farmer go! — Let the farmer go! — Let the farmer go!"

(I guess somebody saw the "Indiana" on Sir Davi's license plate and figured my usual means of transportation was a plow horse.)

At any rate, it looked like I was still headed for jail, until another man walked up with the lady, whom I wouldn't try to save again for a hundred dollars! She sat in a nearby folding chair; and while two other ladies came up to fool with her lips and hair, this new fellow put his arm around the shoulder of the short guy and took him aside for a moment. The crowd buzzed about this latest development, and the officers (who seemed like nice enough fellows to me) loosened their grip. When the two men turned back toward us, the short one seemed to have calmed down a bit, and the other one waved the officers away from me. This stay of execution pleased the people of the Jefferson Street Jury, and they let loose with a thunderous combination of applause and laughter.

The short man walked away with the lady. The officers told everybody to go home, and the man who had saved my skin waved me to walk with him back to the burning building.

Even though when I drove onto the scene I hadn't noticed the big camera near the crowd, I realized I had blundered onto a Hollywood moving picture set the instant the director hollered, "Cut!" I had certainly made a fool of myself; and I was fortunate that this man, the producer of the moving picture, had seen a bit of light-hearted lunacy in what I had tried to do.

As we entered the building, he yelled upstairs to somebody to cut the fire; and no sooner had he ordered it, the flames and smoke that had been pouring from the second story windows ceased. Seeing my amazement, he said, "It's all from metal drums up there . . . you know . . . typical Hollywood hokeyness." He introduced himself as Kyle Martin; and after finding out that he'd grown up around Tell City, I practically felt like we knew each other.

He told me that the deal he had made with the director to keep me out of jail involved helping the crew on the picture relocate the fire scene to a more neighborhood-like area of town. This was the last day the inner-city police would allow them to shoot film downtown; and since I had ruined it all, I considered myself more than lucky to be able to try and make up for it. Kyle wouldn't explain my duties in any detail at that time, but he did say that I would probably catch at least a glimpse of the picture's star.

When I told him that I had already seen enough of her, and she'd already seen enough of me, too, he said, "You mean the lady in the fire? Holy cow, she's no star! No wonder you didn't know why Mr. Allen was so mad! This is his first big directing job, and for this picture we've got the biggest name in the business! He'll be arriving on the early train tomorrow, so be here to help us move the props at 5:30 sharp!"

As he walked away, curiosity struck again, and I had to know the answer to just one question.

"Are you talking about the biggest name in the business?"

He stopped and turned around, but didn't speak. He just pointed his feet outward, twitched his nose, and twirled the fingers of his right hand as though he were spinning a cane. I couldn't believe it. This was going to be incredible.

I drove around town until I found a "Y" that also had a garage for Sir Davi, and well into the early hours of morning I lay awake trying to think of what I would say if I actually had the chance to speak to Mr. Chaplin.

"Howdy, Mr. Chaplin!" Too country.

"Hi, Charlie!" Too informal.

"Hello, Mr. Chaplin, my aunt and I have seen all your pictures!" Too much of a lie. I wanted to see them all, but you and I both know that only about half of the pictures Hollywood ever makes gets to the Louisville theaters.

I finally went to sleep with the decision that if I did see him, I wouldn't act country, I wouldn't be informal, and I wouldn't lie about anything — I'd just have to do my best.

I got up extra early, and my Rider's Workout started me off on what I knew would be a very long day. I wanted to be sure and get back to Jefferson Street with plenty of time to spare, so a quick piece of toast was all I had for breakfast. Before hurrying out to the garage for Sir Davi, I asked the cook for a few extra napkins; and as I passed the registration desk, I asked the man if he'd sell me some pencils. They were a penny each, and I bought four, one for each pocket. With that, I felt as ready as I could be, so I fired up Sir Davi and headed for Jefferson Street.

It was still only a quarter-to-five when I pulled up in front of the abandoned old building, and the electric street lamps cast long shadows into its broken-out windows, making it look haunted. Everything was very quiet; and for a moment, the quiet caught my attention. Thinking back to the rush of people and deafening traffic during the light of the day before, the calm twilight air held a wonderful stillness that made it possible to somehow forget that I was deep within a city that sheltered more people than any other on the face of the Earth. I must say it was sad to think of so many of them — with countless fantastic stories of their own to tell — and know that we have such a short time to share our lives with so few.

But dwelling there on it further made me think of something else . . . that maybe we're supposed to truly know, and help, only a few people in our lives. Spreading ourselves too thin never seems to do much for anybody.

I sat on the steps of a condemned building and wondered who had lived there. All of the other buildings on Jefferson looked to be of the same type — large apartment dwellings — and now a sign had been put up on each one of them saying that "For the Progress of Man, and the Great City of New York, This Building has been Condemned. Do Not Enter — by Order of The City of New York."

The more I looked at the buildings, and the more I thought of what the signs said, I couldn't help but wonder who or what the great city of New York really was. Surely the families who lived here weren't part of the city. They couldn't be. Why would they be a part of ordering their own home torn down? These buildings were in bad shape, no doubt about it; but when the barn down the road needs a new roof, we don't tear down the walls! I guess there's just a lot more to city life than I'll ever understand.

Around five o'clock the traffic out on Harper's Boulevard began to get heavy and a truck turned onto Jefferson and stopped across the street from where I was sitting. A man got out, stretched and yawned loudly, and then yelled over to me.

"Are you Bidwell?"

I called back that I was, and he motioned me to come over. When I got to him, he was leaning into the open window of the truck; and he pulled out a paper bag from off the seat.

"Name's Herbert," he mumbled. "Want some Jacks?"

He had stuffed his mouth full of Cracker Jacks and held the bag out to me. The toast I had earlier hadn't done much for me, so I reached in and took a handful.

Aunt Victoria, you know how I love a Hershey's, and I'd certainly be looking to buy one someplace later that day, but these Cracker Jacks were something to behold. In all my days as a muncher of Jacks, I'd never had any like these!

The popcorn was not only fresh, but the peanuts were as though they had just been shelled and roasted. And the caramel . . . The caramel was as smooth and sweet as if it had just been poured across the stuff that very morning.

Well, my facial reaction to the first mouthful prompted Herbert to give me the whole bag, and I gladly took it. As it turned out, it really had been made that morning! While I stuffed in one handful after another, Herbert explained that his brother-in-law was a manager at the local Jacks factory, and he didn't mind Herbert stopping in now and then to get a sampling of that day's batch.

After I'd pretty well satisfied my current hunger, Herbert caught me with the same embarrassing thing he said he gets everybody with. I had begun to study the inside of the bag closely and was moving the Cracker Jacks around with my fingers when he grinned and said, "They don't put them little surprises in paper bags!"

He'd caught me all right, and we both had a good laugh about it. I could see that if I was to be hard at work that day, I'd run into a good-natured fellow for a boss. He said we had to have the fire scene equipment loaded up and carted off to another spot by one o'clock; so after a couple of other workers arrived, we got down to work. After loading the truck with as much as we could, I followed the crew out to the new set location on Sir Davi and parked him under a tree. After that, I rode with another of the crew back and forth to pick up the rest.

I wasn't able to talk with Herbert again until lunch because we all worked our tails off to get everything moved. The big drums that held the fuel for the fire were some of the heaviest things I've ever pushed around, and it took four of us to get each one loaded onto the truck.

We also had to take down lights, move furniture, and even carefully tear down a wall in the building that would need to be completely rebuilt on the new site by that afternoon!

The men of the crew called themselves "roustabouts"; and they were some of the non-stoppingest, hardest-working fellows I've ever seen. They were all skilled carpenters and electricians, but I don't think they were paid enough. I say that because Herbert had told me that I would get full roustabout pay of $6.25 for the day's work, and I have little or no construction talents at all! These men were in shabby clothes, and working hand in hand with motion picture stars. I'd sure like to know who they'd get to do that kind of work if those fellows ever decided to leave.

The location was on the outskirts of town; and with sore muscles and sweat, the burning building scene was re-set on time. In a mere six hours or so, we moved it all from 15 miles away and had put it back together. People from all around the area had seen what was happening, and crowds were gathering in several different locations along the street in hopes of seeing whatever part of Hollywood they could. I was dog-tired; and as I sat for a lunch break with Herbert and the rest of the crew, a Buick rolled up and the girl, the producer, and the director got out. The director looked my way; and even though he still had his dark glasses on, I could easily imagine the look he was giving me from behind them. He took one look at the road, and called Herbert to come over for a minute. As they talked, the director pointed to a few different spots on the road and then motioned in my direction. I didn't know what it was about, but soon enough Herbert jogged back to our group to fill us in.

"The boss says we've got to be sure and keep the crowds back all up and down this road today. There'll be some fast scenes with the fire wagons and he don't want any accidents. Everybody got it?"

I said, "Sure," right along with everybody else. But then he added, "Well, that's not your job, Harmon. Mr. Allen has something else for you to do."

"Right," I thought. Like stand behind the horses to make sure they don't kick somebody innocent? Or use a lighted match to see if the fuel drums are full?

I could only imagine what lovely chore I was about to be gifted with by the ever-thoughtful Mr. Allen. Herbert came back, picked up a shovel, and handed it to me.

"Wants me to dig my own grave first, right?"

"No, he's not bad once you get to know him. He wants you to take this and fill up those holes in the road as best you can. None of us wants to see Mr. Chaplin thrown from a wagon today, and taking care of the holes would be a big help."

I felt pretty bad thinking that Mr. Allen would stay mad at me forever, and now I had been given a task that would put me in a position to maybe catch a glimpse of Charlie Chaplin! He wasn't supposed to arrive for a while yet, but there was this invisible kind of excitement all around that I can't explain, but you could feel it. Somebody opened up a large crate and pulled out the most expensive Edison I'd ever seen. In no time at all, Joplin's latest melodies poured from the horn, and the whole working atmosphere was alive with it. I asked Herbert if the crews always worked to music, and he said they did, but it wasn't always to Joplin. "Mr. Chaplin picks the music for the theater piano players, and he likes to hear it while the film is being shot so he can put himself in the same mood the audience will be in when they sit and watch the finished film." After hearing that, it occurred to me that Mr. Chaplin must have a lot more to do with his films than just be the star we're all used to seeing up on the screen. I took my shovel and began walking away and was glad to hear "Alexander's Ragtime Band" on the Edison. I love that one and can't wait to see where Mr. Chaplin wants it played during the picture. Herbert told me the film's title is The Fireman, and I'm sure it will be yet another fine collection of hilarious Chaplin chaos.

Finding ten times the number of holes I expected, I began filling them up with loose gravel and dirt from the side of the road. (It was in that gravel that I spotted an unusual kind of crystal that I've never seen in Indiana, so I'm sending it back for our collection.) There were a lot of places in need of repair, and I worked as fast as I could to be finished before Mr. Chaplin arrived on the set. I was sure that he'd be driven up in some kind of extra-expensive auto and everyone would crowd around close to get his autograph, and I didn't want to miss that!

Looking at the number of holes, and having no one to help me fill them in, made me all of a sudden realize that maybe Mr. Allen wasn't such a forgiving soul after all. It was beginning to be obvious that I'd be shoveling for the rest of the day and would miss any real chance to see Mr. Chaplin. I wasn't really even sure that the road I had been put to work on would be used in the motion picture at all! There were a couple of roads that wound around the building for the fire scene, and I was now fairly certain I had been sent off to be completely out of the way.

A little while later, Herbert drove up to check on my progress and brought me a cola and a Hershey's. I had told him at lunchtime how much I liked them; and he said that if he could get away for a minute, he'd pick them up for me. I thanked him, but then said I had an extra favor to ask of him if he didn't mind. He agreed to help me if he could, and then drove away. I went back to shoveling and had worked my way around a curve when shouts and loud cheers thundered from the crowds, making it obvious Mr. Chaplin had, in fact, arrived. I was tempted to drop the tool right there and then, but a fire wagon full of frenzied firemen came wildly swerving down the road, and I saw several more large holes that needed attention.

Whether or not I would get my chance to see Charlie Chaplin was set aside in my mind because I had accepted the job; and even if this road was just a back road to be used by others, I needed to finish it.

Aunt, what happened only a moment or two later I can scarcely describe, but it's certainly worth a try to re-tell.

I could all at once smell smoke; and when I turned, I could see the second-story window of the building above the trees. The crew had successfully restarted the fire on the new set, and it looked real enough to be a four-alarmer! From out of nowhere an older gentleman in a nice suit came running toward me, and at the same time a flat-bed truck came speeding around the corner. There was a man with a large camera on the back of the truck, and Mr. Allen was up there with him screaming to the driver, "Wrong road you fool! You're on the wrong road!" Then he pointed to me and yelled in the cameraman's ear, "I don't care if that idiot gets in the picture, keep rolling! Keep rolling!!"

The man in the suit practically knocked me down, asked me if I'd seen any firemen, and then went running off in the other direction. Mr. Allen's truck went flying by, and over at the scene of the fire I could hear all kinds of commotion going on. Water was shooting higher than the trees, crowds were shouting, sirens were blaring . . . and through clearings in the brush I could see firemen, autos, wagons, and horses racing about at the same time in every direction!

Figuring something must have drastically gone wrong, I decided to quickly finish filling the hole I was on and run back to see if I could help. But I had no sooner made this decision when the camera-truck reappeared and stopped in the same spot it had before. Mr. Allen hollered for me to get out of the way; but before I could move, a fire wagon swerved around the other corner and came barreling down the road.

"Not again!!" I heard the director scream. And then . . . "Keep rolling!

This is it!! Roll it! Roll it!!!"

As the wagon straightened up from its slide around the corner, I understood why these shots were so important to Mr. Allen, for there behind the reins of the stampeding animals was the timid tramp himself: Charlie Chaplin.

His wagon careened wildly, and he didn't look big enough to be riding a child's pony, let alone taking charge of two huge horses; but he was doing it all the same. He glanced my way for a split second as he flew by and flashed a smile, and I somehow knew that one instant in time would be our only meeting.

I finished up the holes and then ran back to the building. The crowds were no longer there, and the crews had already removed most of the lights and equipment used for the filming of the scene. Only a smoldering of the once thick smoke drifted from the windows, and a few tired horses stood here and there drinking water from buckets. I had, indeed, missed it all.

The producer, the director, Herbert, — anybody I would have recognized — was gone. I walked to Sir Davi, and there on the seat was a brown paper bag. I knew what was in it, and I said out loud, "Thanks, Herbert!" I sat on the seat and opened it to get a handful of the Jacks that I knew were still going to taste fresher than any from a box; and when I reached inside, I felt something. . . and pulled it out. It was an envelope, and on the outside was a note:

Harmon,

We roustabouts had to pack up and go. Next stop for us is St. Louis. You did a good job, and your pay is enclosed. Hope you enjoy the Jacks — and don't stop looking for the toy surprises!

Herbert

It was getting late in the day, and I thought I'd drive aways out of the city's limits before resting for the evening. I opened my knapsack and took out my goggles, scarf, and jacket; and before putting the Cracker Jacks down inside for safe keeping, I reached in the bag for one more handful.

I felt something else down inside it, off to one side and covered with several layers of the candy. It was soft; and when I pulled it out, a few pieces of carameled corn were sticking to it. I brushed them away; and when I turned it over, I could see that Herbert had found the time to do me the favor I had asked of him.

It was one of the napkins that I had hurriedly stuck in my pocket at breakfast, hoping by some impossible chance that I would get Mr. Chaplin's autograph. It was creased, dirty, and now sticky as well; but the handwriting that had been added to it was completely legible, and said:

Harmon,

Often our roughest roads are smoothened by those we never know. You made mine a little easier.

Thank you,
Charles Chaplin

I'd like to keep it with me, Aunt Victoria, to show it to others when I share the story along the way. But if any of the ladies at the garden club won't take your word for it, buy them seats for Mr. Chaplin's next motion picture. Seeing will be believing!

Love,
Harmon

Because students experience the film through this letter before they actually watch it, their mindset is to see it in precisely the same way Harmon did!

A very compelling illusion, but what of its academic applications?

Of the many inquiries involved with this letter, one of the most dramatic has been the focus on the incredible power music has in association with our emotions. Music can make us happy. Music can make us sad. It can make us buy, it can make us sell. Ironically, its range of possibilities through infinite melodies may be the only thing that can match our equally infinite range of emotions. Maybe that's why we call on it so often to fit or soothe a particular mood. At any rate, my kids have always thoroughly enjoyed our time spent with activities involving music and emotion. One such activity is The Silent Film.

> Here is one way the power of music can help create a special feeling on film. All you need to do is film the faces of classmates for the time allowed. Then listen to the Silent Film Music as you watch your film. Music is powerful indeed!

Sixth-grader Angie Johns (with clap board) displays great patience as she attempts to direct her classmates in a silent film.

1. Film the sign, "One Day at School," for 5 seconds.
2. Film students looking sinister for 10 seconds.
3. Film the class happily busy at work for 48 seconds.
4. Film students with terror in their eyes for 35 seconds.
5. Film classmates in love for 46 seconds.
6. Film expressions of great sorrow for 48 seconds.
7. Film heroic poses for 15 seconds.
8. Film the sign, "The End," for 10 seconds.

You now have a short silent film of many emotions!
Watch it with the sound on the TV turned all the way down
and, if possible, turn off the color too! Your teacher has a
special collection of actual silent film music to accompany
the film. Enjoy!

For students, the process of completing this very quick film is
funny enough, but the result is always nothing short of hilarious.
I play the director; and I receive some unexplained enjoyment
from hollering like one, too. One kid holds the script (the activity sheet above), another holds a stopwatch, and a third uses the
video camera. Since the 'actors' have nothing to say, there's nothing to memorize or practice, and everyone readily participates.
As you might expect, some giggles surface from the 'sinister
group' during their few seconds of being on camera, and the same
thing can sometimes happen during other moments of "sadness"
or "terror." But undoubtedly the most memorable scenes caught
on film are those involving love. Hand holding and the "down on
one knee stuff" are as far as we get, but it still brings down the
house every time.

As the class watches the film, the cassette with the silent film
piano score is played. I simply recorded timed bits of the required
music to match the emotions that were to be filmed by the camera
person. Even when we have paid very close attention to be sure the
camera person filmed students only for the amount of time allowed
for each emotion, it never fails that the playback of the finished
film and the playing of the cassette in a nearby tape recorder are
out of sync by at least a second or two. But no matter. The result is
an even more hilarious overlap of "sinister" piano music playing

during a love scene, and the students' overall understanding and appreciation of the moods music can create or enhance remain with them long after this simple inquiry is finished.

When students have been watching films completely unrelated to the Harmon program, they will turn to me in the dimness of the room and whisper, "I think that spider is about to get eaten by that bird."

"How come?" I whisper back.

"Because of that screechy way they're playing those violins in the background."

"Ohhh," I say.

Chomp! No more spider.

That tense violin might have been a tip-off for anyone, Harmon activity or not. But students who more carefully consider the vast range of music that is constantly aimed our way in order to influence us are ahead in the game of being taken in by clever manipulation. That's why we extend this activity to the observance of TV commercials and how the advertisement industry uses particular music (or its unusual absence) to capture our attention and affect our judgment of a product.

I'd like to add that one more item I like to do with the Charlie Chaplin films is to play one with the TV completely turned away from the students' view. All they can do is listen to the film's accompanying piano music.

It is very interesting to see them listen intently (how often do kids listen intently?) then raise their hands to tell me what they believe the action on the screen must be at that same moment. It's neat to hear them piece together a story that follows the changes in the types of music they hear; and, once again, they become very aware of the role specific melodies play in creating desired moods in finished presentations.

In returning our thoughts to Harmon's letter about his chance encounter with Charlie Chaplin, what else do we find among its pages that may serve as springboards in the classroom? Every letter has an association with some kind of food or snack, and the Cracker Jack connection in this letter has lead to a world of interesting tidbits. To name a few, we have: The Cracker Jack Time Line, Cracker Jack Recipes, Make a Cracker Jack Toy, Write a Tiny Cracker Jack Storybook (to be placed in a large Cracker Jack box in the room), Write and record a Cracker Jack Commercial, and others.

After being inspired by Harmon's awe-stricken view of the extreme height of the skyscrapers in New York, one teacher created an inquiry that had students build scale replicas of the nation's tallest skyscrapers at that time.

This letter is short in comparison to most of Harmon's others, but there are no doubt many other activities that can be pulled from it, with every one easily linked to specific state standards. Perhaps someday I shall hear from a reader who has spotted a "hidden" inquiry in the letter that simply cannot be left out of students' hands.

When Harmon made the jump from the "Twilight Zone" and became as old as he should be chronologically, he brought with him the possibility of having somehow experienced anything imaginable from the entire 20th century. And this led to one of the most enjoyable bits of writing I have ever put together.

Earlier, I mentioned the fact that the Beatles were inserted into Harmon's travels. Obviously, they weren't around in 1916; but if you knew of my personal appreciation for their contribution to the world in the form of poetry and music, you'd understand why there was no way I could leave them out. In truth, only one Beatle is entwined into the story; and even then, his mania days of the 1960s play no part. But having just one Beatle seemingly added the creativity of them all, and I was very happy to hear the folks at Columbia Recordings state that I could use a particular Paul McCartney music video in the program as long as it didn't involve selling it.

In 1986, I happened to see his creation about an unusual occurrence during World War One. It seems that in 1914, the British and Germans (in one particular area of the devastation) decided to stop fighting for a single day. It was Christmas Day; and at the determined hour, guns were silenced. Battle weary, yet hopeful men slowly emerged from the filth of the trenches on both sides of a secluded field. They met in the middle and, after exchanging chocolates, liquor, cigarettes, and even photos from home, a muddy football (soccer) match was soon under way after one soldier produced a ragged ball.

The scene's total absurdity reflected that of the war itself, and McCartney's incredible accompanying song, "Pipes of Piece," perfectly lays before the viewer a vivid sense of the senseless. After seeing this short film a single time, I knew the event had to somehow cross Harmon's path. And when the idea came to me about just how that would be done, I delighted in its contrivance.

After being the fortunate recipient of the Christa McAuliffe Fellowship in 1995, I took one semester off from school and set out to write Harmon's continuance of his travels beyond the United States. This new journey took him to France to become a pilot. Thus his eventual involvement with the enemy and the students' introduction to excellent poetry in song were on a collision course.

Once again, I found myself discovering nothing that could not be written into a story for deep inquiry by students. Harmon's letters had become "The Travels of Harmon Bidwell," for his writings were no longer directed to his Aunt Victoria but were now a diary of sorts. He titled his works, "Thoughts for a Book by Harmon Bidwell," yet he states within that he never fully expects to see it become an actual book.

Of course, Seth has a different idea. Along with the original letters, Seth has acquired most of his grandfather's stories and poems from France. Without his grandfather's knowledge, he pieces together Harmon's adventure abroad.

It is a story, according to Harmon himself, that has no real title. (At least, it doesn't surface until late in the telling.) It is a story with chapters, but with no names for them, either. (It's up to students to create chapter names after reading and discussing each one.) And it is a tale that continues the "Harmon style" of leaving many opportunities for teachers to stop and discuss or to activate an inquiry.

As you read the following few pages of the story's beginning, think about what might be submerged beneath the print, waiting to surface.

Thoughts for a Book by Harmon Bidwell

How do people write books?

And more than that, how do people write good ones?

I've questioned myself often on it lately — for I've considered trying to write one of my own — and have come to the conclusion that there must be more to it than it seems.

One thing, though, that to me stands right out, is importance of some kind. Good books have something of use to share with people. Now, I'd be the first to admit that what's important to one person might not mean a thing to someone else. But when there's a general acceptance among most folks that a book has a useful purpose, that book can be called a good one.

The most important thing in my life up to this point has been a "who" really, not a thing, and she would be my Aunt Victoria. I lived with her for years, and she had her own way of finding out what was and what wasn't important.

Anytime she found herself headed for some kind of decision-making situation, out came the paper and pen, and down would go a list.

The ladies coming after church for tea? A perfect list-making occasion. Cups, spoons, ice, napkins, cookies, chairs, even where everyone would sit!

An afternoon drive with Mr. Cook in his latest auto? Another list. This one was made after she'd spent hours reading a road map, and it would have on it all of the towns they'd pass through during the day. I suppose it was usually a fine thing to have, but more than once I recall her coming home aggravated with Mr. Cook for making a wrong turn and driving straight through an unlisted town.

But when it came to the one she most thoroughly mulled over, making sure nothing was forgotten and everything on it was placed to perfection, none other compared to the weekly organization of the grocery list. I watched it being made out at least a hundred times, yet marveled anew at its creation on each and every occasion.

Everything in place and always neatly alphabetized, from asparagus to zucchini. Aunt Victoria took more pride in her gro-

cery lists than all others, and was often noticeably annoyed at the fact that grocers could not somehow manage to organize the wares on their shelves in equal fashion.

My life spent with her from the age of eight to nearly twenty was apparently plenty of time for her list-making ways to rub themselves off on me, for it is in that manner that I expect to come up with what must be important and what might not be so important to make up a book, and hopefully a good one. I'm not sure it will work, but at least it's a way to get me started; and something is telling me I need to write while I'm here . . . but not in a diary.

Diaries, like letters, aren't meant to be read by more than one person. No, I'd like to write a book.

A book for the kind of schoolchildren whom I one day hope to teach. And may it be a story that somehow helps them learn that the way they get along with others when they are children is very much the way their nation will make its way among the world of nations when they are adults. Today, the nations of the world are at war — millions have been lost — and I have found myself among the devastation. I haven't been too awfully scared yet, but then again, I've only been here 15 days and the tasks assigned me in that time have kept my mind from what I know lies ahead.

Writing has helped me see my way through times of trial before, so I hope that here it may well serve the same purpose once more . . . and supposing that if what I write may someday be published, I would like it to be known that this story is dedicated to anyone who dedicates themselves to peaceful existence with others. So, as inspired by my list-making aunt, here is what I hope to include in this, my first-ever book:

Love,
Characters of Unusual Nature,
Real Places,
Made-up Places,
A Dedication Part (that one's finished)
Ferocious Beasts,

Friendly Beasts,
A Table of Contents,
Music,
A Map,
New Discoveries,
A Lady in Distress,
A Hero,
A Title,
Excitement,
Something Frightening,
Mystery . . . and
A Happy Ending.

At least some of those things could be found in every story I ever heard of; so the way I see it, if I can fit them all somewhere in this book, it's bound to be a good one!

I left an empty page up front and put some numbers on it. The reason was so when I write a chapter, I can think up a name for it, go back to that page, and write the name down.

Seems to me as easy as any a way to make up a good table of contents; and if after a chapter is finished I can't think of anything to call it, it can just stay a number until I do. Besides, I don't think what they're called means nearly as much as what they're made up of. But as for a title . . . a title needs to be something bold and noteworthy.

"Thoughts for a Book by Harmon Bidwell" is certainly no title; but until I come up with a real one, it'll do.

And speaking of doing, Maurice the cook just rang the mess duty bell, and my name's on the list.

This book will have to wait.

Anything in there? Of course there is! I believe we all see particular sets of hidden possibilities. You may have thought of something involving musical intelligence, or perhaps an intrapersonal inquiry came to mind. When I wrote it, it was obvious there would be the usual highlighting of the common elements of reading curricula, namely standard vocabulary stuff and comprehension; but I also enjoyed the idea of having the story have a lot of incomplete factors as well, things on which kids could expand with the least guidance possible. Thus, the "list of things" idea.

As I've read aloud this part of the saga, a large copy of Harmon's list is on the wall, and students have consistently (and usually politely) interrupted me in the middle of a line to say, "Right there! That's got to be the part that goes with his list when he said he wanted to include 'a friendly beast'!" The list concept works well as a way to help keep a high level of attention and anticipation, and the leaving out of names and titles for things holds even more fascination. I think this is true because kids like to see adults making mistakes, or at least find adults midway (and often struggling) through the process of creating new things. Intentionally writing such mistakes, or designing "unfinished work" into inquiries we develop, leads to chances for children to feel the encouraging effects of participation and creative originality.

Harmon left the following one untitled, and the intrapersonal feelings it stirs within students make for great discussions. I often take out some of the "We all like . . ." lines from the middle and have them write their own, and they always come up with classics. But what would you choose for its title?

It's possible to be alone in where you choose to wander,
and you can be the only one who lives there in your home.
But you should also realize, my friends, there are a number,
of very special ways that you are never all alone.

You're not the only one who thinks the world is growing smaller.
You're not the only one the lightning's thunder ever shook.
Your teeth, your face, your hair, your eyes, your longing to
*   grow taller,*
you're not the only one who'd like to change the way they
*   look.*
We all like starry summer skies.
We all like full moons on the rise.
We all like hearing eagles' cries.

We all like anyone who tries.
We all like getting valentines.
We all like holding kites with lines.
We all like aromatic pines.
We all like those who think we're fine.
We all like skipping smooth flat stones.
We all like popping bubbles blown.
We all like finally going home.
So many ways. . . we're not alone!
So, if we're all so much alike, why do we go on fighting?
It seems we have so many things in common we can share.
And those uncommon ways we are just make life more exciting.
Be glad that we're all different . . . for we're each beyond
    compare!

CHAPTER 4

FUNDING THE ADVENTURE

Transferring an adventure from your mind to paper is one thing, but finding the money for activities and materials can be quite another. I suppose I could list a hundred or so corporations that support education in general; and if you wrote to, say, fifty of them, perhaps you would receive a thousand dollars or more. It might be worthwhile, and I have certainly spent a lot of time hammering out one proposal after another.

But after eight years with Harmon, I have finally realized that "funding" has many sources and comes in many forms. In fact, it has flowed most freely and abundantly through active participation.

One of the earliest instances of this was during our first year. I simply had to have a real barbershop quartet for the talent fair. I found one, and they cost $125 for three songs! I suppose this instance would not be so clear in my mind had they at least dressed for the part. That's right, they wore regular clothes, not their matching striped suits and hats; and one of them couldn't even wait until he'd left the presence of the students before smoking a cigarette! Needless to say, I was fairly aggravated as I witnessed their performance through binoculars from my hiding place. We had raised their fee by having each participating school chip in, and I resolved to never have the possibility of such a performance happen again. The solution came as one of those "Why didn't I think of that before?" realizations, followed by smacking my own forehead. Since then, it blossomed into a hilarious act that has been immensely enjoyed by everyone every year.

"Ladies and Gentleman, put your hands together and give a rousing Lanesville Talent Fair welcome to . . . The Harrison County Hummingbirds! Singing bass: Mike Carter. Singing alto: James Kendall and David Kaiser. And stepping out with lead tenor: Mr. Tom Huckaby. Today's song, that old-time favorite, 'Wait Till the Sun Shines, Nellie'!"

The crowd loves it; the "singers" have a great time; and oddly enough, no matter what the distraction, they never miss a note. (Neither does the assistant behind the stage who plays the cassette right on cue.)

Even though students sometimes realize (actually, they rarely guess) that the song is being lip-synched, the effect is perfect. So is the cost. It requires only the participation of interested friends.

Without my friends, a project as large as Harmon would have ended after its first run. I owe a tremendous debt of thanks to so many, and I'll certainly include the names of many more friends, as well as their contributions, later. However, not everyone who sponsored the journey has wound up on stage.

One day, Tim, one of my sixth-grade boys, walked into the classroom spinning an odd looking toy he had received after buying a Happy Meal at McDonald's. It was the size and shape of a small, round, margarine container. It had a dozen, evenly spaced vertical slots cut into it. Inside, a single strip of paper had 12 tiny drawings of a running horse, with each drawing depicting a slightly different stage of the animal's stride. As the cylinder spun, Tim's friends immediately swarmed him, amazed at the apparent live action of the horse in full gallop. I neatly confiscated the thing as a toy that didn't belong at school!

Of course, in reality, I took it with Tim's understanding that I, too, was fascinated by it and that I would give it back when I was finished playing with it.

That same day, I visited several McDonald's locations. To my disappointment, none of the "Animation Wheels" were still available. I didn't realize that Tim had acquired his own a few weeks earlier, and McDonald's had discontinued the item. I took that to mean that they'd stopped handing them out, but there had to be some more hiding somewhere!

One of the store managers gave me the name and phone number of the regional McDonald's manager in Indianapolis. After describing Harmon's tale for 20 minutes, I was told where to pick up a donation of 500 Animation Wheels in Bloomington, Indiana. The manager shared with me that they were the "very last of all the wheels available." They quickly became an exciting part of studying the history of the moving picture and were a special hands-on accompaniment to Letter #4 with Charlie Chaplin!

The success of acquiring the Animation Wheels was matched time and again. As I shared Harmon's tale with potential contributors to the program, I learned that quickly getting to the point was vital. Soon I was able to give the gist of Harmon's entire adventure in around 12 minutes.

It was amazing just how many people were willing to assist in a program they would never actually see, and at least four sponsors come to mind who were roughly a thousand miles from the students they were helping.

Contacting the Planter's Corporation in South Carolina resulted in hundreds of packages of LifeSavers being mailed to me, and 400 Hershey's Bars showed up on my doorstep for several years in a row after I reached the right person at the Hershey's Corporation in Pennsylvania. In the early days of the program, I wanted the original 11 classrooms to have metal windmills to accompany Letter #1 and to use when studying how to build a tower, so the Woodbine Manufacturing Company in Iowa granted my request by sending along an eight-foot windmill for each class.

Rocket building is one of the most motivating elements of Harmon's journey. Having Harmon reluctantly meet and assist rocket pioneer Robert Goddard in Letter #3 was an obvious contrivance to insert student-constructed rockets, and the Estes Company in Colorado came through with high-flying colors when they donated more than 400 rocket kits to the cause!

On board the Belle of Louisville riverboat, which Lee Cable once piloted, members of the Harmon adventure pose for students. Shown are (left to right) Lee Cable, Irvin Brewer (the author's father), the author (as Harmon), and his brother, Kyle.

By far, the most concentrated effort to bring community sponsorship into the 'Harmonized' classroom was through the thought to fix a few cats.

It was the third year of the program. Seventeen schools were involved; and somehow I decided to have each classroom have the chance to get one cat spayed or neutered free of cost. I called the first veterinarian my finger landed on in the Yellow Pages and talked for 12 minutes. One down, 16 to go! It took a while, but eventually I was able to get the 17 vets needed to donate one free operation for each class.

The premise was that the students would study the vets' hand-outs on pet population explosion and then discuss the disasters of letting cats and dogs multiply. Finally, students obtained permission from their parents to have their cat's name thrown into the hat, and a drawing was held.

Of course, for some reason Harmon had written home about cats; and in his eighth letter, he has just picked up two hot-air balloonists whose balloon has crashed. One is named Captain Dan Silverstein, and he is accompanied by his deaf brother, Albert. All three of them have managed to squeeze themselves onto Sir Davi, and Harmon has just precariously steered them onto the long gravel driveway leading to the Silverstein home.

It was a big orangish-colored cat . . . and with its long body lying stretched out across a good bit of the narrow roadway, I had but one choice, and I applied both of Sir Davi's brakes with more force than I ever had before. In an instant, I knew what the result would be, but there was no way to avoid it. Sir Davi's wheels stopped cold, and it skidded uncontrollably. The combined weight of the three of us was pitched to one side and then to the other as six outstretched legs flew about, wildly groping for earth in an attempt to somehow keep us from taking a nasty spill in the loose gravel.

It was no use.

We managed to miss the cat by a few inches, but spun off the drive and down over a short grassy slope near a pond, where we were all thrown bronco-style from our mount. I wound up flat on my back, looking straight up into the blue. And turning my head to the side, I saw Albert sitting up laughing in silence and pointing at his brother, who hadn't been pitched into the pond, but rather had fallen just short of it and landed in the blackish, cattail-filled muck at its edge. I was sure that this would outrage the captain to the point of fighting with his brother right then and there, but I was wrong. Dan kept his humor, raised his slime-coated arms, and, with green water sloshing from his boot tops, he dragged himself out, laughing, and said, "At least it was a soft landing!"

I was glad to find that the only damage Sir Davi had sustained was a slight crumpling of the fuel tank and was further relieved to discover it hadn't caused any leaks. I pulled him up and rolled him back onto his stand with a quiet, "Sorry 'bout that!"

All at once I remembered the cat and ran back up the slope to the road. "Oh No!" I thought sadly. I hadn't missed it after all — for there in the drive the cat rolled violently from left to right, back and forth, over and over in obvious pain. With no idea what to do, I knelt beside it.

It made no sound, and there were no signs of blood, making me believe I'd severely injured it internally. I was certain it was a fatal injury as well because time and time again I'd seen animals struck by autos on my travels, and the result was often this same horrible contorting of the body, followed shortly thereafter by death.

The captain and Albert were only now making their way back up to where the animal and I were; and when they arrived and saw what I was looking down upon, the captain said, "If mother didn't love that cat so much, I'd send him to the middle of that pond to get a taste of what he did to me!" Albert soundlessly laughed again and made his way walking up the drive to the house. The cat still lay flailing about, and I looked up at the captain in sheer disbelief at what I'd heard.

"You mean this is your mother's cat? . . . and she loves it, too? Oh my gosh!" The very seriousness of my tone caught him off guard, and he seemed not to know what to say; but then his eyes widened and he let go with another laugh, saying, "You don't think we ran over Bakersfield, do you?

"That idiot cat is always pulling that stunt! He's not hurt; give him another minute and he'll be off frolickin' with every other blasted cat mother's taken in from this side of Tibet!"

I knew he was wrong, and I couldn't believe he was being so harsh to a terribly injured animal. I decided right then I was taking Bakersfield to the nearest veterinary doctor, with or without this so called "captain's" permission, and that I had no desire to return to this "lovely" home for any type of further contact with people of this sort. I gently placed my hands under the still-shaking cat's huge furriness and had no sooner begun to gently lift him when he suddenly stopped thrashing about and leaped from my grip, bounding away toward the house with all the life of a frisky kitten!

"Told you so," said the captain.

"I don't know what gets into him and some of those others, but believe me, its a regular wild west show when it comes to cats around here."

The captain's words were sort of . . . well, "give in" kind of sounding, like he didn't really want to have a bunch of cats around, but there didn't seem to be much he could do about it for some reason.

He called out "Mother!?" as we approached the steps of the huge front porch; and at the sound of his voice, at least six rather thin-looking felines of various sizes and colors scampered away through the railing off the far end. The old stained glass in the tall front door rattled as it swung open, and there stood a very kindly looking woman. Where her long checkered dress touched the floor stood two more cats. One, a Siamese of some sort, stood still at her right, while the other, a long-haired white cat of unrecognizable breed, rubbed itself briskly on her left leg. Thinking back on it now, neither one of those animals had a particularly healthy look about it; but at the time I didn't pay too much attention to it. I was soon to find out, however, how little attention the Silversteins paid to it as well.

The inside of the home was simply beautiful, and Mrs. Silverstein proved to be as warm a hostess as she appeared. I was invited to stay for the evening and gladly accepted. I had, after all, not had a good bath for too long a time. And after a grand supper, I went to my room upstairs and was delighted to find it had its own bathroom connected to it. Not only that, the Silversteins were wealthy enough to have a maid who worked at the home throughout the evening hours of the day, and she prepared plenty of water for a wonderfully steaming bath. In less than half an hour I'd carried enough up, and it was "heaven on earth" to slip into a nearly overflowing tub of hot soapy water. With my head laid back on the rim, it was impossible not to drift off to sleep, and I did just that — soaking to the point of wrinkling myself to what looked to be a 175-pound raisin

I would most likely have stayed there all night but was stirred awake, what must have been hours later, by the loud spits and moans of a cat fight below my window.

Later, as I tried to sleep, the scratching and loud hissing of one fight after another woke me several more times deep in the night, and I wondered why it was really necessary for Mrs. Silverstein to keep so many cats around.

I discovered the answer early the next morning as Captain Dan, Albert, and I were sitting at the breakfast table. Mrs. Silverstein was in the kitchen; and when I asked the captain if he'd heard all the racket the night before, he said, "Sure I did, and mother's already got the veterinary doctor on the way. I guess one of them got cut up pretty bad, and she's worried sick about it. But . . ." he leaned my way and said in a lowered voice, "We might want to get ourselves out of here and up in the Hoopskirt before he arrives!"

"Why?" I asked.

Albert was seated across the table from us and he knew what the captain was trying to tell me, so he pantomimed the whole scene out for me. First he acted like he was stroking the fur of a cat in his arms, protecting it with outstretched elbows. "Yup! That's mother!" said Dan.

Then Albert straightened up, stuck out his chest a bit proudly, and walked in a quick circle. In his hand he gripped some kind of imaginary suitcase, and he pointed to where his mother character would have been, holding the cat.

"Hey!, that's a good Doctor Styder, Albert!" laughed his brother, but Albert didn't hear him, of course, and kept up the act. As best I can describe the rest of the scene, Albert played his mother one minute, sheltering the cat from the wicked doctor, and the next moment became the doctor trying silently to explain that he was a good man and knew what was best for the animal.

The tension mounted when Albert (as the doctor) picked up a butter knife, pulled the imaginary cat from the straining woman's arms, and suddenly became the cat himself. He made hissing expressions and flicked his fingernails like claws, but it was no use. With his feet stretched apart and his left arm outstretched as well, he held the dull butter knife in his right hand and slowly let it glide on his shirt from his chest to his stomach, his "cat face" agonizing at every inch of the imaginary cut. At last his head dropped to one side, and his tongue hung out, dead as a cat can get. As a final depressing sight, Albert sprang a few feet from where he was, to turn back into his mother one last time; and he buried his sobbing face into his hands and turned from the evil doctor, crying bitterly as he walked away.

Throughout this whole incredible act, I'd caught myself laughing as quietly as I could right along with the captain. Neither one of us wanted Mrs. Silverstein to come out from the kitchen and see Albert making fun of one of her cats. But the more I thought about it, the more I realized I'd just been laughing at Albert's actions; and I really hadn't considered what in the world the whole thing was about. Captain Dan must have been reading my wondering mind because, as Albert plopped into the seat next to him with a wide grin, Dan told me the story.

"Every time one of mother's cats has a problem — and there have been lots of 'em — she sends for Doc Styder; and it never fails that when he arrives, he does his best to talk mother into letting him cut the whole lot of them open and take out some of their . . . you know, 'special parts'."

He looked at me sort of like a teacher does sometimes, wondering if I knew what he meant by "special parts."

I knew what he meant. I'd just never heard of a cat's reproductive system being called "special parts" before. Anyway, he kept talking.

"Well, mother won't even act like she hears him when he starts up with that, and she shoos him away just as soon as he's doctored up whatever the ailment is. I don't really mind the animals, but I'm beginning to think she keeps a few too many around."

"Just how many cats does she keep here?" I asked.

"41."

"41?!" I could hardly repeat the number without shouting it.

"Quiet!," he said. (Even the captain's usual booming voice was down to a near whisper.) "If mother hears you say that, she'll know were out here talking about her cats; and that could rile her up real quick. That's just the way Doc Styder talks about them, except he gets even worse. The last time they got in to it, he actually said she was hurtin' her animals more than she was helping them! When I heard him say that, I nearly busted him a good one; but I stopped myself at the last second for thinkin' about there's no other veterinary doctor around these parts who could get here when mother needed them fast. No, I just gave him a look that he knows meant he'd best not talk that way with her again! Mother means the world to Albert and me; and even though she loves us as good as any mother could, we know she has a special place in her heart for animals, especially cats. Why, people all over town know it, too. And maybe that's what started the problem. It seemed that for a long time, just about every week somebody new was bringing her a kitten or two; and she couldn't seem to say no to keeping 'em. It didn't appear to be much trouble at first — you know, with kittens being as cute and silly as they can be — but in no time at all the kittens were gone and full-sized cats stepped up and took their place! You know, as I remember it, it was only last spring we were feeding 10 or 12 around here. But now? Brother! Forty-one and still counting more every time we turn around."

The captain laughed a bit to himself, but I could tell there was really nothing very funny to him about the situation.

Mrs. Silverstein came through the door of the kitchen, and we were quiet. She squeezed onto the edge of Albert's chair and sat across from me between her two boys.

"Doctor Styder will be showing up soon, boys, to check up on that nasty scratch above Fluffy's eye; so call me as soon as you see his auto." She gave both sons a kiss and, as she got up to leave, added, "And I do hope he can give Bakersfield something for those awful convulsions! Sometimes I think that cat will just tie himself up in a knot and stay that way!"

She left the room chuckling to herself about what she'd said, and it made me remember the awful way the big orange cat had twisted and thrown itself about on the driveway. Its miraculous recovery still puzzled me, and I wanted to ask the doctor about it when he arrived, but I never got the chance.

I believe this passage clearly illustrates the endless possibilities for the insertion of selected topics into the curriculum and also demonstrates how a sponsor's useful contributions can be included, even if such a contribution doesn't happen to match with any preset curriculum. When the opportunity arises that we can add something of unusual value for students to experience, we need to adjust the current curriculum so that it can be used.

The handouts the veterinarians provided were read and discussed in classrooms, and the homemade certificate proved valid enough, as cats were spayed or neutered as a result of the vets' participation.

Of course, not every large corporation or local business that I've contacted over the years has been in the position to supply students with specific materials or services, but dozens have donated financial assistance in place of them. For a few years, simply thanking these contributors was my primary means of showing my appreciation. But it occurred to me that there was a much better, much more inclusive way to do so.

My daughter, Jennifer, just missed being in the first sixth-grade class to enjoy Harmon's journey. But she eventually played a major role in the experience students have at the annual talent fair.

By the time she was a freshman at the high school, (which is only 50 feet from the elementary school) she already was a fine writer. This led to her becoming the editor of the school's newspaper, and it was natural for me to latch on to her for the production and publication of the *Laconia Gazette*, our official talent fair newspaper.

Our own local newspaper, the *Corydon Democrat*, gives us a break on the printing of the 500 copies we order each year, thus making the *Democrat* another player among the long list of sponsors.

The fictional *Gazette* offers great opportunities to have fun, as well as to take care of business. On the front page, which features a story about the historic farm we were thankful to be using, I throw in a ridiculous picture and article about the Harrison County Hummingbirds. Dozens of photographs of students enjoying fairs of past years fill the pages; and the large, middle-page spread displays pictures of all of the financial contributors to the program, as well as a list of those who are assistants in many other, unique ways.

Looking at the sheer number and variety of ads from the *Gazette* makes me realize just how involved community and corporate sponsors like to be, especially when it comes to contributing to an enriching experience for children!

There was one other way in which sponsorship for the program was attained. That was through radio commercials written by the students.

It was great fun to introduce Harmon to the world of radio in Letter #6, when he finds himself (along with Sir Davi) on a ship heading south from Delaware to South Carolina. One night, he is in the wheel house with the ship's owner, Admiral Irvin.

Last night, as we were watching the faint lights of yet another town drift slowly northward, what I thought was a screech owl suddenly ripped the complete stillness of the night with a piercing scream.

The admiral was standing at his post at the wheel and didn't flinch a muscle, but I nearly jumped through the closest window.

"What in the good Lord's world is that?!" were the first words I heard coming from my mouth, as I kept myself bent low to keep whatever had flown through one of the opened windows from crashing in to me.

The admiral reached over and picked up a small, rounded piece of metal. It had a long wire attached to it, and the other end was sticking into a hole in a box. He turned a switch on the box, and Aunt Victoria, with the Lord as my witness, a man's voice came through it!

Not only that, but the admiral talked to him!

After the general shock of what I had seen and heard wore down a bit, the admiral let me talk to the man myself. And talk we did.

The man's name was Franklin McCormick, and he spent hours telling me all about the new, upcoming world of wireless talking. It's called "radio," and he told me that he worked for a radio building in Pittsburgh.

He was talking to me from the coastal town of Myrtle Beach, South Carolina, where his mother lived. His father had recently passed away, and he had left his job and home in Pittsburgh to come back and help his mother. He hoped to be able to return to Pittsburgh soon because, he said, the government was about to give the radio building the official permission to begin transmitting radio signals out to anyone who had a receiver to pick them up. He sometimes called it a radio "station" and said it would be known by the four letters, KDKA. He said that when he left the station, his boss wanted him to come back with something "new," something fresh that future listeners would want to hear. Not just a sports report, not more news reporting. They would always be needed, but his boss wanted something more.

I could tell from the excitement in his voice that Franklin would somehow get back someday; but for now, he would be with his mother and the small amount of radio equipment that he brought to Myrtle Beach with him.

He explained that it was strong enough only to reach anyone else in town who may have their own receiver or to reach passing ships on the ocean. He enjoyed talking with anyone who would talk with him, and he knew the schedules of many ships that were traveling up and down the coast. That's why he blasted a signal of radio static in our direction. He knew that the Hartwell would be passing through; and he had spoken with Admiral Irvin on other occasions, until the ship sailed beyond the distance the radio would allow each other's voices to be heard. Franklin told me that lots of shipping companies could afford to have radio equipment, and they were beginning to see a great value for it. But as far as everyday people on land were concerned, most of them had never seen a receiver before, and many still had not even heard of such a thing.

Needless to say, Franklin and I talked until sunrise. I had told him about you, Sir Davi, my trip, the people I've met, and what I used to get for Christmas. He shared with me the latest about his dreams for what he called a coming explosion for the world of radio. He told me of his father, his plans to marry his sweetheart in Pittsburgh, and what he used to get for Christmas. Ironically, at one time he had a toy Merrimac, and he could hardly believe it when I told him of Donald Irvin, the cabin boy. By the time we were finished, the admiral had been relieved by Riley, and I was simply too tired to talk anymore.

I slept until nearly two in the afternoon today, and I was delighted to find that we had dropped anchor five miles south of Myrtle Beach to wait for a smaller boat to bring out an added shipment of goods to be taken down to Charleston by the Hartwell. The admiral told me that we would stay anchored for tonight and then make it to Charleston in the morning.

I've grown plenty weary of the deck washing, knotting, and salt-air breathing life of a sailor. But at least following supper tonight, I should have one more chance to talk with Franklin. I've got work to do now, so I'll have to wait until morning to finish this letter.

11:00 in the morning, December 21
For the second day in a row, I've slept very late. The mates on board don't seem to mind though, because I worked extra long after supper last night. It was after 10:00 last night, and well below freezing by the time I'd finished my duties. The cook gave me a cup of hot chocolate and said that the admiral had called down on the galley horn for a cup as well. I walked the winding steps up to the steering house and, even before reaching it, I could hear the admiral talking to Franklin on the radio. When I came through the door, he turned the speaker over to me and took his cup.

The chocolate in my cup had sort of thickened at the top, so I found a stiff wire and stirred it up a bit as I greeted Franklin. His first words back to me were, "What's wrong with your engine?"

"My engine? You mean the Hartwell's engines?"

The admiral heard Franklin's question, and looked to me and said there wasn't any engine trouble.

"The admiral says there's no problem here," I said as I continued to stir my drink.

"Then what is that clunking sound?" he asked.

I suddenly realized the "clunking engine" Franklin heard was the wire banging up against the sides of my cup as I stirred my hot chocolate!

I looked to the admiral, who was grinning, and started stirring faster.

"You're right, Franklin, engine trouble! Admiral! number one's about to blow!

I stirred as wildly as I could and made the best mouth explosion I could into the speaker.

"Wow! " came back Franklin's voice. "You guys okay?!?"

The admiral and I had to hold our mouths to keep from bursting.

I stirred hard again.

"Admiral!", I called, and this time he joined in, "Oh no, Bidwell! Number two's just about gone!"

"Skaaa - Booooooozzh!"

This time we couldn't hold back, and both the admiral and I broke loose with loud, long laughter. When we finally quit, I listened for Franklin on the other end. All was silent.

"Franklin? Okay, I'm sorry. It was just a joke. Where are you? Say something. We apologize."

No answer. I thought I'd really made him mad or that maybe he had actually run off someplace to report a ship in distress. But a moment later I heard his out-of-breath voice come from the box, and he said, "Okay, it took me a while to find something, but try this one!"

"Do what?" I asked.

"Tell me what this sounds like," he said.

The admiral and I found ourselves leaning toward the box, listening as closely as we could. When we heard the sound of an egg cracking, I said, "It's kind of late in the day for breakfast, isn't it?"

Franklin let out a whoop that was part laughter, part sheer excitement. "That wasn't an egg! Did it really sound like one?"

"It sure did," I said. "What was it?" He didn't answer. He was gone from the radio again. He returned a moment later, saying, "Here! Here's another one! What's this?"

The admiral and I stared in wonder at each other as Franklin spoke from what sounded like the inside of a cave. "How'd you do that?" I asked. I heard his speaker hit the floor as he ran off to find something else.

Well, Aunt Victoria, the admiral had long gone off to bed before Franklin and I stopped making sounds at each other throughout the night. Riley came on duty; and after he saw what was going on, he even came up with a couple himself. (My favorite was when Riley took a big bite of an apple up close to the speaker. Franklin swore Riley was twisting my head right off my shoulders to get that sound!)

We didn't stop until the Hartwell neared the point where Franklin and I could tell we would soon lose radio contact. The box began to make occasional hissing sounds; and not being able to hear each other well, we shouted through the speakers. We decided the last thing we would share would be each other's mailing addresses. And when we were through writing them down, Franklin called out, "and if you're ever in Pittsburgh, tune in to my radio broadcast! Remember, it's station K - D . . ." and then, silence. The Hartwell was beyond the limit.

Perhaps someone will soon find a way to make voices carry in the air as far as they do on wires. Now that would be something!

Uh oh. Admiral Irvin just called through the horn that we'll dock in Charleston in twenty minutes, and Riley just stopped by to say he wants me to tie the ropes that will hoist Sir Davi ashore.

I can do it. I've had good teachers.

I'm sorry to cut this letter so short, but things here are happening fast!

Have a wonderful Christmas, and I'll be thinking of you and everybody else who always stop by Christmas Eve before church for a piece of your pumpkin pie. Let Mr. Willard have my piece, and I'll just go for doubles when I get back!

Merry Christmas Again!
Love, Harmon

Although there are many types of multiple intelligence inquiries that go well with this letter (examples include tying knots for kinesthetic intelligence or comparing miles per hour to knots for logical/mathematical), what certainly stands out is the fact that the marvel of radio must be addressed. And that idea has community and corporate sponsorship written all over it.

We all know that most kids love making noise. In fact, teachers spend a good deal of our day in failed attempts to get some students to stop disrupting the class with their noises. Everything from tapping pencils to squeaking chairs can annoy even the most tolerant of us. But if there ever was an inquiry that would captivate those "sound-off" types of learners, it is the simple production of an old-time radio show.

Such an activity encourages students to be constructively noisy by creating sound effects. The results are often highly creative and always entertaining.

With Admiral Irvin (Irvin Brewer) at the wheel, young Harmon is fascinated by his first experience with radio.

Community sponsors greatly enjoy hearing their company's name in the script and have called me on several occasions to personally share their delight at the simple student commercials inserted during the program. Such commercials have earned the class anywhere from $25 to $100, and often they have taken only minutes to write. Sound effects are a must in such advertisements, and the sponsors are made aware of the fact that students read about the history of radio, write their own scripts, and practice the art of expressively performing them.

Two special stipulations I like to throw in are that no commercial may be a copy of an existing one — neither in text nor tune — and that our ads should reflect the flavor of the old-time show we are re-creating. In other words, if students are doing an ad for Bennett and Bennett Insurance, the commercial should have lines in it that make it sound like a 1920s Bennett and Bennett ad would sound. Do the sponsors like such "outdated" stuff? Very much!

Here's my favorite way to introduce the class to the magic of sound effects:

First, I look through the house (or our classroom) for any odd junk that might be sitting around. Virtually anything can be used for a sound effect of some kind. The last time I did this with kids, I think I had a toothbrush, a piece of sandpaper, some pencils, a glass jar, a roll of Scotch tape, a spoon, a box of toothpicks, and who knows what else. (It absolutely doesn't matter!)

Next, in the classroom, I make sure I have something to kneel behind so that the kids won't see what I pull out of the box. Sometimes I just turn a table on its side and get behind it.

Then I start making noise! Using one object at a time, or sometimes using two or more together in some weird way, I rattle, shake, thump, twist, squeeze — whatever the objects allow — to make all kinds of sounds. Soft ones, loud ones, repetitions — anything. And the kids always amaze me. By not seeing what's making the sound, their brains kick in; and they listen. Really listen. And think hard, too. As they lean forward and cock their heads to the side, they begin to name things that the sounds resemble: "A truck with squeaky brakes!" "No, no. That's a typewriter!" "Wait a minute! That one sounded like water dripping into a bucket from a gutter!" "No it's not! It's that ancient 'Pong' game my dad has down in the basement!" "Whoa! That was pants ripping. Who ripped their pants?"

As fun as it is to hear and see them using their imaginations, it's just as much fun to see the expressions on their faces when the actual, simple devices that created the sounds are revealed. This opens their eyes to the fact that radio can easily create vivid imagery. It also reveals that they can create their own sounds. Their first task is to select and practice sound effects from a list of suggestions and to practice ones they come up with themselves. As you'd expect, the kids often come up with better and more realistic effects than those found on the list. A few from that list are:

1. Airplane: Hold stiff cardboard against a battery-powered fan. For a jet, turn on a vacuum cleaner.
2. Animals: Use your voice to imitate a cat, cow, dog, and horse whinny. For horse hooves, clap coconut halves onto a hard surface.
3. Arrow: Swish a stick through the air. For the hit on the target, strike a firm surface with the palm of the hand. For the twang effect, hold a ruler firmly on a desk, allowing most of it to hang over the edge. Flick the ruler and allow it to vibrate.
4. Baby Crying: A high pitched voice muffled by a pillow.
5. Baseball Hit with a Bat: Strike a thick, hollow piece of wood with another piece of wood.
6. Bird Wings Flapping: Flap flat pieces of canvas near the microphone.
7. Blood Pressure Gauge: Rapidly squeeze an atomizer with your finger over the end of the nozzle.
8. Boat Rowing: Dip a wooden paddle into a tub of water or lightly blow through a straw into a glass of water in a rhythmic fashion.
9. Bones Rattling: Suspend wooden sticks on strings to a board, then clank them together.
10. Breaking Bones: Chew a LifeSaver close to the microphone or snap thin dowel rods wrapped in soft paper.

11. Bottle Opening: Press two plungers together and pull suddenly apart or open your mouth and snap your cheek with your finger.
12. Breaking Eggs: Take a six-inch square of coarse sandpaper. Lay it in the hand rough side up, and suddenly squeeze.
13. Breeze: Cut sections of newspaper into long strips and wave close to the microphone.
14. Brook Babbling: Blow air through a straw into a glass of water. Try various amounts of water and blowing at different speeds.
15. Camera Click: Snap the switch on a flashlight.
16. Coal Cars: Roller skates on a piece of iron.
17. Cow Being Milked: Squirt water into an empty metal container.
18. Creaks: Twist and squeeze a Dixie cup close to the microphone.
19. Crickets: Run a fingernail along the edge of a fine-tooth comb. Make the sound loud, then soft.
20. Digging: Fill a small wooden box with several inches of dirt and a few rocks. Use a fireplace scoop or small shovel and force into the dirt at an angle.

Once students have practiced sounds from the list or those they thought of themselves, we work on the basics of writing good commercials. I like to point out to students that because they are creating radio commercials, it is extra important for them to choose their words carefully. Their time on the air is limited, usually from 20 to 30 seconds. Within that time, every word is of great value.

As excellent examples, we listen to classic radio shows, such as Abbott and Costello, Jack Benny, or Franklin McCormick's "Jack Armstrong, the All American Boy." The stories shared by these characters are enlightening enough and create abundant opportunities for teachers to insert lessons focused on clever humor and superior presentation skills. However, when close attention is paid to the delivery of the many commercials in these broadcasts, there is the added bonus of improving students' active listening skills and helping them to become constructive critics of their own choices of words.

To my best recollection, every student has participated in writing commercials. Everyone understands from the beginning that a commercial script, even a very brief one, must be written down before a recording will be made of the ad and its sound effects. The incentive to write for such a performance gets even the weakest of writers to collaborate. It's simply too appealing to students to make noise in a microphone. And after they've witnessed me having fun playing with the sound effects, it's never been tough to get creative writing from even those students who often portray language arts as a near-death experience.

Finally, we're ready to put it all together using the following basic radio show script. I use the same script with students in my graduate education class, "Encouraging Creative Curriculum," at Indiana University Southeast. As you might expect, they are bigger hams than my sixth-graders!

Live Radio Script

Opening Announcer: The National Broadcasting Company and _____ is proud to present "Meet the Makers," the weekly broadcast that brings you the people behind the scenes who make the big stars shine! And now, here's your host for "Meet the Makers," _____!

Host: Thank you, _____, and welcome to the show, everybody! We certainly have a very special guest on this week's "Meet the Makers." I'm sure you've all heard much of the work that he (she) has been doing lately, and I do mean heard the work! That's because we have for you tonight *the* biggest name in radio sound effects. And that, of course, is _____! Welcome, _____, to "Meet the Makers."

Sound Effects Expert: Thank you, _____. And thank you for having me on the show.

Host: Our pleasure, _____. You know, lots of

folks enjoy radio's sound effects as much as they do their favorite stories or music. Why do you think that's true?

Sound Effects Expert: Well, I think it's because it leaves so much to the imagination. When a sound effect really does its job in a story, it makes it all much more real to everybody listening, and that makes it more exciting and fun, too.

Host: It sure does. And don't forget sometimes frightening as well!

Sound Effects Expert: Oh, definitely! A good ghost on a show can really send the chills up a listener's spine.

Host: And a fresh broken egg on a head can bring down the house! Well, our listeners are really in for a treat tonight because you've brought a whole bag full of special things for us.

Sound Effects Expert: Yes I have, and I think we'll have a lot of fun together letting all of you out there in radio land listen to a variety of sound effects we use on our many NBC shows every week.

Host: Okay, we're going to let you create the sound, and we'll let everybody at home use their imagination. Then we'll talk a little bit about when that sound might be used in a radio show. _____, do we want to tell the people listening what kinds of things are really making these sounds?

Sound Effects Expert: Well, _____, we can tell them what some of them are if you'd like. I don't think NBC will get too angry with us for letting out a few tricks of the trade. But perhaps we can keep some a secret.

Host: Sounds great! Are we ready?

Sound Effects Expert: Here we go! (begin making sounds)

(The teacher should make sure that students are lined up with their various sound effects, ready to get close to the microphone when it is their turn. Remind them to do their sound effects loudly.)

(The broadcasters should ad-lib. Make comments between each new sound effect. This isn't always easy to do, but it is one of the things good radio broadcasters learn to do. Silence doesn't work on radio.)

(Don't forget that, midway through the show, the announcer or announcers do a commercial for your sponsor. After the commercial, complete the show with your own script, or use the following ending.)

Host: All right, we're back with our very special guest, _____, here on "Meet the Makers." We have time for just a few more great sound effects!

(After all of the sounds have been made, the host can finish the show.)

Host: We'd like to thank _____, one of NBC's greatest sound effects creators, for being on this week's edition of "Meet the Makers." As always, we'd like to thank _____ (sponsor) for bringing you our show.

This is your host, _____, saying goodbye and reminding you to be sure to tune in next week when the National Broadcasting System will once again let you "Meet the Makers"!

The greatest payoff for students who enthusiastically write and perform radio show ads often comes on the day of the talent fair.

Those who put serious effort into their work (and many do) are given a spot in the day's lineup to get up on stage, lean into the microphone on cue, and take us reeling back to radio days. You can well imagine, I'm sure, the effect such a live commercial has on a sponsor who is standing among hundreds of kids in the crowd on that day!

Sponsorship from small, local businesses, as well as that from larger corporations, is a wonderful thing. The results of such school/community relationships always are exciting and create authentic incentives in the classroom. The work produced by students in such cases very often reaches levels that are stunning to these sponsors, making the links between the business world and the classroom a priceless, as well as endless, set of possibilities through which the creative instructor may greatly enhance both the academic abilities and life skills of young learners.

CHAPTER 5

THE PILOT

From the moment Harmon sprang into existence in my mind, I had a vision of a large number of students taking part in the adventure. I never actually considered just how many students would eventually participate, and I still have no precise count of those who have done so. But over the past eight years, with 25 to 35 teachers participating each year, the number must be somewhere around 5,000.

New teachers are added every year. They do not learn about the project from a school directive. Rather, they learn about it in a manner that I believe is best for such a project: word of mouth.

I have two requirements for teachers who wish to join Harmon's adventures, and they are the same requirements I have had from the beginning. The first is that the teacher must truly enjoy reading aloud to kids. The second is that the teacher must have a desire to participate actively right alongside his or her students in all kinds of (sometimes slightly crazy) activities.

Unfortunately, these two requirements leave out too many teachers. All of us could make lengthy lists of the teachers who don't like to get up and do things. But for Harmon's Travels to reach their potential with students, the teachers must be actively involved with rocket launches, radio shows, making silent films, the Rider's Workout, and pyramid kite flying. The teacher also must be willing to read to students, and to do so expressively. It is disturbing how seldom quality reading is shared with children of all ages.

Because I have a strong belief in the importance of reading aloud to students, I took care to ensure that the first Harmon teachers would be outstanding examples of instructors who still had something left in them from the great bedtime stories enjoyed as a child. While there is a long list of such teachers in the Harmon project, I want to mention Irvin Goldstein.

Professional makeup artist Kelly Yurko turns the author into a 100-year-old man.

I laughed out loud when Mr. G. came to mind as being one of the first to share Harmon, probably because I could so vividly see him still reading aloud with fantastic realism to his students, just as he had to his students a quarter-century earlier. At that time, he probably looked up from his book no less than a dozen times a day; casting firm glances toward some disruptive, spindly, sixth-grade numbskull who had no clue at the time of the special attention with which he and his fellow classmates were being showered.

Today, I am slightly less spindly, but the memories of listening to "Rikki Tikki Tavi," *A Cricket in Times Square*, and countless episodes of Encyclopedia Brown instilled in me the continuing need to hear a great reader read a good story.

It was Mr. Goldstein's final official year in the classroom. Retirement awaited, but Mr. G. would make his last year one of

Harmon's best ones. I knew he would. It was an obvious choice to have him on board, and I was sure that other teachers I wanted would not be as hesitant to give "this new Harmon thing" a shot once I mentioned that Mr. Goldstein was with us.

Retirement came, but it didn't keep Mr. G. from coming back. The next year, he was invited by the new teacher to return to Slate Run Elementary to read the letters once again, creating an experience that I well know will long remain with those very fortunate children. Even the disruptive spindly one.

All of the teachers who have taken their students on Harmon's adventure have enjoyed support for the program from their principals. But first those principals had to be convinced.

In those early days, I conducted some rather passionate inservice programs for the teachers. Many of them have told me that, after hearing me describe his tale, they felt as if Harmon was alive and that they vividly saw how he could be used to help their students, both in and out of the classroom. They took this enthusiasm back to their principals.

Soon Harmon's letters made their way into the hands of teachers from one end of Indiana to the other. One teacher would share the tale with another, and I would receive a call inquiring about how one might join. My first question then remains the same one I first ask today: "Who told you?" If the answer is that they have spoken directly to a teacher in the program or, better yet, have visited a classroom where Harmon is being used, my response is usually quick and to the point: "Of course you can have it!" If their school is close by, I simply take them my master copy of the huge teacher's manual. They have three days to copy and return it.

A simple, but noteworthy thing to consider if you ever do the same with your own materials is to be sure to place your pages in plastic covers. When I discovered that even my plastic-covered work was somehow getting out of place in the manual, I inquired about it and found that some of the teachers were letting others on the staff actually do the copying. Now I have a note on the front that says, "Copy this yourself!" Keep in mind that no one cares about your creations as much as you do.

A missing page or two is trivial. But the problem I had a few years ago, though very small, was a bit harder to take. If you design a curriculum that leaves your classroom and finds its way into the hands of teachers in other schools, you might do well to take note of the following.

I was very fortunate that among the first teachers I invited to pilot Harmon's letters was one who dearly loved to read to her students and to incorporate all kinds of good things in the classroom. She was even more enthusiastic than the other teachers I asked to try it, and she did an amazing job with the materials. However, news travels fast on a playground. Soon a few parents called the school to find out why their kids, who were in other classes, had not been given the chance to participate.

I had never considered such a problem. Kids who were not in the piloting teacher's class were not going to be exposed to a program designed to be delivered by highly enthusiastic instructors. The result was a principal caught in the middle and children on the losing end. The teacher in question was given the materials but was very reluctant to do it justice.

I was fully on that teacher's side. Who would want to have someone come in and say, "Get ready. You are starting this thing tomorrow!" I know I would not take kindly to some untested program being forced on me. I had no inkling at the time that the adventure might cause uninterested teachers to become involved. Since then, I have taken huge steps to ensure that it does not happen that way again.

When a teacher in another town called and asked me to come to the school to share everything with her and the principal, I was overly cautious. Thus, when I entered the conference room and found six teachers, the first words that came out of my mouth were, "You need to realize this will not work if there is anyone here who was prodded into participation." I suppose I was tired. I speak bluntly when I'm worn out, and my curtness surprised the group. However, it was a point that I wanted to be understood plainly. To my relief, the original contact teacher assured me that all six teachers were very willing; and that was, indeed, the case.

But I continue to be cautious. That first "failed" experience has taught me that the teachers who participate in this type of program must be enthusiastic volunteers.

If teachers are not enthusiastic, their students lose in two critical ways. First, the teacher might not take the initiative to inject even the simplest, quickest inquiries between the lines of the letters. Second, these same teacher's students are left to discover just how much other kids are being immersed in the journey by more enthusiastic teachers.

The author's own students had trouble recognizing him after he had been "aged" to 100 years.

CHAPTER 6

INCLUDING OURSELVES IN THE ACTION

In the fall of 1973, I played in my last high school football game. For me, football was a daily challenge for survival, and I was good at it. Knowing just when to get a drink of water or to run to the bathroom was an art that saved me more than once from being lined up face to face with the likes of a Mike Carter or David Kaiser during tackling practice. To the best of my memory I never actually faked an injury to get out of such a thing; but then again, I don't have the best of memories.

However, I very distinctly remember the night that I decided I would go out for the ninth-grade team four years earlier. More than that, I remember why. All of my best friends played — yes, Dave and Mike among them — and it was those two and so many other close friends who made the game what it was for me.

In my junior year, I took on a great affection for punting, which was most likely another survival technique. The pleasure I got from booting a ball beyond the reach of the vicious people who were attacking me led to a two-year stint as a kicker at a junior college in California. I eventually got good enough to be accepted as a walk-on at Indiana University. But things catch up to you when you're merely a survivor; and, as so many minor-league athletes find, I was suddenly surrounded by much larger folks.

Even their punters resembled tackles. It quickly became obvious that I would never again feel "game grass" under my feet. I finished spring practice with the team in 1977 and turned in my uniform.

Up to that point, kicking footballs was the only reason I had even considered going to college. Now my thoughts turned to trying to pass the classes to which I had previously paid little or no attention. One of those classes was called Elementary Logic; and to me, it was the furthest thing from it.

It was a course that Mr. Spock probably would have dropped for fear of failing. But I dredged my way onward, always hoping that the next class meeting might be the one where I would finally comprehend what was going on. Of course, I never did. But one day, as the instructor was somewhere in the middle of another bizarre explanation about explaining explanations, I suddenly, momentarily, understood something. It was called modus ponens, and goes like this:

If A, then B
A, therefore B

This simple, two-line insight continues to inspire me to inspire teachers. I recall it every time I share the manner in which Harmon Bidwell came to be.

The statement seems simple. But if we make a proposition and plug it in, see what happens.

If kids love learning, then we love teaching.

Do you agree? It's incredibly easy to love teaching when we look around and see a room full of kids excitedly engaged in active learning. If they truly love learning, then we unquestionably have an easy time loving teaching.

But don't forget how modus ponens works! If kids love learning, then we love teaching only takes care of line 1. *If* is an important two-letter word. What makes kids love learning? We cannot simply go to line two of the statement:

Kids love learning. Therefore we love teaching.

You can easily see that the second, or concluding, line assumes far too much.

Don't get me wrong. I believe that all kids love to learn. But I have also taught long enough to know that using the word love when describing a child's affection for standard textbook-based curriculum is absurd. Though it would be nice to love teaching simply because the kids *first* loved learning, we can throw this one out.

But we certainly can try to change a few lines to reach validity. What if we change the order of the statement?

> If we love teaching, then kids love learning.

When we happen to discover or create lessons in which we lose ourselves, lessons that provide us with so much personal excitement, then kids love the learning. They can't help but love it, because they respect and love us. And when those moments end, we stop and mentally replay them, saying to ourselves, "Wow! That one worked!" But once again, there is a problem when we see that second, flatly stated line.

> We love teaching. Therefore kids love learning.

As before, we are assuming too much. Of course, we have those fantastic moments when we feel a sincere love of the profession. But when those incredible times happen with too much distance between them, the inspiration to teach dynamically is too tough to maintain. None of us absolutely love what we do all of the time. But any teacher who has experienced a great love for a lesson and has seen its reflection in the students' eyes wants that to happen for those kids as often as possible.

So what's the solution? I would never go so far as to say that I have such a thing. However, I do have a suggestion. I call it *inclusion*. When we add this line to the above statements, something true results.

> If we include ourselves, then we love teaching.
> If we love teaching, then kids love learning.
> We include ourselves! Therefore we love teaching.
> We love teaching. Therefore kids love learning.

Those first eight words define the past eight years of my life as Harmon Bidwell. Hundreds of thousands of self-selected words, countless hours spent in writing volumes of interrelated inquiries, and scores of special, personal relationships woven into an adventure that could take any twist or turn to include any new idea.

There was and continues to be an overwhelming feeling of satisfaction in knowing that students are learning from a work that was created from my personal love of writing, playing and listening to music, constructing things, appreciating great achievements in history, physical activity, reading, and so much more.

Master of Ceremonies Jerry Cook prepares to announce the "Best-Dressed Teacher of 1917."

The large number of inquiries that have been included have been successful with regular and gifted students. Teachers of special needs children also have told me that their students participated in these same inquiries with an extremely high degree of fascination. I credit this simply to the personal nature with which Harmon communicates to his aunt, a feeling I was able to write only when I allowed myself to enjoy the memories of my own past and to write them as they naturally would be spoken.

Without a doubt, the most entertaining element of a self-created curriculum is the imaginative insertion of almost whatever one wishes to include. But another delight of the self-constructed adventure comes with the addition of that which perhaps only you will ever know about. That is, you will be the only one to know only if you do not tell your students about it.

The exposure of Harmon was something I never considered in the first few years. Why would I? I could ruin everything. That turned out to be nonsense; and Maxwell Monts, a sixth-grade teacher at Clear Creek Elementary School in Bloomington, Indiana, proved it to me. In 1998, Max called and said he wanted "closure" for students in the adventure, a definitive end. He invited me to reveal Harmon's true identity in his classroom.

I appeared in the doorway as 100-year-old Harmon, complete with name tag supplied by the office. For the first fascinating half-hour, the kids riddled me with every question they could think of, either out of sheer curiosity or possibly to test my knowledge of such a journey. As its author, I was impossible to stump; and even the serious doubters were completely baffled by the raspy-voiced character before them! I even shared a few favored tunes on a banjo Max had found. Then the time arrived for the unveiling. This was quite a literal thing, too.

Max announced, "Class, this is Mr. Neil Brewer. Like me, he teaches sixth-graders. He is Harmon, and he wrote the story we've been enjoying since Christmas."

I reached just below my collar line to grasp the edges of the heavily wrinkled latex mask that had been heat formed to my face. Then I slowly began pulling it off in one large plasticene sheet.

The disbelieving shrieks from a few prompted me to stop for a moment, leaving the lower half of the mask hanging from nose and cheeks. And then, speaking for the first time in my own voice, I again stunned all onlookers with an, "Ouch, I hate it when this stuff sticks to my mustache and eyelashes!" The finishing touch was achieved by dropping the wadded-up face of Harmon Bidwell into the lap of an obviously good-humored girl in the front row.

I had believed that Harmon's reality was the magic for the young travelers. But since that day, I have been convinced that the greatest magic is in sharing the fantasy. Ironically, years earlier, it was Max who had made a statement that I have always taken as the greatest compliment the program ever received. Hundreds of kids had unexpectedly rushed to meet me as I pushed Sir Davi across that open field; and at an opportune moment, Max quietly said, "Neil, you've re-created Santa Claus!"

Doing such a thing was never my intention. But there were, and continue to be, thousands of kids who have lived through the adventure never knowing of Harmon's fictional standing. Many teachers assured me that the intense interest, concentration, and active participation by students of all ages and academic levels completely justified the means to such an end.

Max Monts was the first to decide to take that ending a step further by revealing Harmon's designer, and I'm glad he did. The questions those kids had for me that day were insightful, and I reveled in the telling. "Who is Seth?" "Where did all those pictures of you come from?" "Why did you choose the name Harmon, or Bidwell?" "Where did the idea for all this come from in the first place?" "We saw Sir Davi in those old photographs. Where is he now?" "Is Aunt Victoria really your Aunt Victoria?" "Harmon was colorblind. Are you colorblind, too?" And my favorite, "How did Harmon get into that Charlie Chaplin film?"

What happened that day has become one of my favorite elements of the entire program, for it has allowed me to share personal inspirations and creativity on a new level. And I have shared it not only with children, but with adults as well, especially through the graduate education course I teach.

Sharing the construction of the journey became another way to include myself in the teaching, and I can assure you that I love doing so. We include ourselves, therefore we love teaching. We love teaching, therefore kids love learning.

It should be remembered that the goal of the curriculum is to involve the students we seek to reach. It just happens to work out nicely that, in doing so, we can make the task of educating one that is highly personalized and enjoyable for both the students and ourselves.

When you create something for students, it will spill over into the lives of others. That is especially the case if you truly take to heart one of the main points of this book and involve your family and friends.

Your family and friends will love getting involved with kids in school. True, that may be because they don't have to deal with students constantly. But that means that their energies will be concentrated on your creation.

There always has been tremendous adult participation with Harmon, and these wonderful assistants have received as much joy from the students' reactions to the program as I have. Their contributions have been extremely varied, ranging from students who buck hay bales to skilled aviators freely providing the expensive use of their biplanes. And every volunteer has given a resounding "Yes!" when asked to do it again the following year.

By far, the largest number of these contributors come together for the annual pilgrimage to Lanesville, Indiana, for the culminating talent fair. But many provide important services to students within the classroom during the weeks and months before the arrival of that exciting finale.

Friends and family often are willing to provide tremendous amounts of work to help develop a project for students. For example, my brother, Kyle Brewer, always found the time to help with all of the photographic aspects, including taking pictures of all of the attending classes posing with Harmon on the day of the fair. Afterward, he would retreat to his basement photo lab and reproduce, at cost, hundreds of copies of these keepsakes for each of the students who wanted one, and they definitely wanted one.

Another key player in communicating the program to students, and to the world, is Charles Moman. To students, parents, and fellow instructors, Charles is an excellent, highly respected teacher of music in Seymour, Indiana. To Harmon Bidwell, Charles is an icon of technical know-how. Charles never turned down any request to assist me with work on Harmon. One example of his work is Harmon's website, which includes a huge assortment of "everything Bidwell." The site includes a historical, photographic introduction by Seth, information on the graduate course credit available from Indiana University Southeast, talent fair photos, student products, letters and poems, a description of Harmon's post-war trek through the 1920s as a freelance newspaper reporter, and the "how-to" for teachers who want to find out about joining the program. Harmon's website address is: http://members.aye.net/~harmon.

A website is simply too powerful a tool to ignore. Students love to see their work and the work of other students on the Internet; and every day more and more of them come to class saying, "We're finally on the net at home!"

Almost every teacher has many friends like Charles and Kyle, people with special know-how who will jump at the chance to be a part of their vision for kids.

So many have played important roles in this project that just to list them all would make a huge book. Therefore I limited this important recognition to a few pages following my final chapter. However, there are a few whose unique contributions made Harmon's story possible. Two of these are Lee and Karen Cable. Karen, a therapeutic artist by profession, painted the sign for "Lee Willard's Restorable Relics" and, dressed in a heavy, full-length dress, patiently allowed me to direct her into the scarf-knitting poses we needed for Kyle's photos of old Aunt Victoria. Hundreds of photos were taken and arranged in a six-minute video that introduced the students to the adventure.

Lee did a magnificent job of portraying Lee Willard, the aging junkman who had sold Harmon the Harley Davidson that would become Sir Davi. Before the project was changed to include an introduction by Seth, it was a short movie of Lee that pulled the students in.

Movies in 1916 would not have included sound. To make the film look old, it was shot in black and white. Also, we added the old-time "click clack" of a movie projector in the background. This sound was achieved by taping an index card on a record turntable spinning at 45 rpm and having the card strike a mounted clothespin with each revolution.

For the feel of an old man's junk shop, Lee and I made the film in a wooden shelter house, piled high with antiques borrowed from everybody's barn and attic. As with any film-making process, there were dozens of outtakes, which ranged from ringing cell phones to screaming 737s. But after four days and 23 takes, we had captured the five minutes of footage necessary to hook students.

There is one other element you will need in large quantities in order to create your own thematic curriculum: Time.

You want music. You want students to move. You want inquiries that involve the right materials. And you want something that somehow connects all of these things, be it a story, a poem, a play, a historic recreation, a film, whatever. No matter what it may be, it will happen only if you have the time to stop and think.

The time you will spend on designing your curriculum will make it easy for you to understand the careful selections I made concerning the first teachers who would experience my work. Those teachers, as well as all the teachers who became involved

After arriving by biplane, Harmon interviews a student at the closing celebrations.

later, have helped the project to evolve. They share ideas with one another, create new inquiries for the overall project, and are constantly in e-mail contact with me to let me know how their students react to related classroom activities, as well as about their students' feelings toward Harmon's actions in the story itself. Such communication between these teachers and me has prompted additional twists and turns for Harmon and Sir Davi on more than one occasion, resulting in the inclusion of the teachers' favorite topics inserted somewhere into the story.

In the following example, sixth-grade teacher Laura McDermott asked me to write a piece that would have Harmon enjoying a rather harrowing device she had introduced to her students for physics. As it just so happened, we were doing a little bit of physics in our sixth-grade classroom as well. The logical blend of these two came to me as the shortest letter Harmon ever wrote.

November 1st, 1916
Dear Aunt,

If my writing appears a bit difficult to read, its cause would be related to the fact that I'm still somewhat rattled and shaking over what I must share with you about last evening.

This being the day that it is, you might guess that my condition is a small leftover from being frightened by those once-a-year spirits who jump from bushes, hang from trees, and generally make themselves sore in the throat shouting for candy while romping through innocent neighborhoods.

But no, I can assure you the goblins and witches who dress up like children for the rest of the year had nothing to do with my torment. They are but fantasies — yet my horror was real! It stood before me as the monstrous beast it was, and its thunderous roar and gargantuan size struck fear into me and all who dared get close enough to feel its terrible grip. Indeed, I screamed louder than the mother and child I was captured with throughout our perilous ordeal, and the simple fact that we all lived to see the sunrise this morning justifies my total belief in guardian angels.

In the event you haven't guessed, I visited famous Palisades Amusement Park last night and was thoroughly thrashed, thrown, terrified — and thrilled — by what has to be the single greatest roller coaster on Earth!

They call it the Cyclone; and believe me, it's name well fits its effect on the mind of those who allow themselves to be swept away on it. At one point I was certain my lungs had removed themselves to settle in somewhere just behind my eyes, while at the same time my heart had changed places with the three hot dogs I'd eaten while waiting in line.

An accurate description of a ride on the Cyclone is fairly easy to write. Here it is:

You get strapped in next to somebody — maybe two somebody's if they are of general size — and when the railcar, (which holds about 20 people) is full, the attendant says, "Everybody stay in your seat!" Then he pulls back a release lever as tall as he is, and you slowly roll down a short hill. You laugh a little. The people around you laugh a little, too. (You later realize this is the last time any of you do that.) You're about to turn to the person's face (which is right next to your own) and say, "Hi" or "This ought to be fun" or something quick and friendly like that, when you and everyone else receives minimal whiplash to the neck as some kind of hook under the railcar grabs onto a giant chain, which slowly pulls the unwary lot of you to the top of a peak so high you fully expect to see those who have died and gone on to lie around on nearby clouds. However, silly thoughts like that soon pass; and as you move skyward, you actually begin to enjoy the diminishing world far below. You see the tops of high trees, tiny people everywhere among the park's booths and other rides, and you notice the many sizes and shapes of never-seen rooftops. And there, as you reach the very top, the saltwater winds fill your nostrils and your breath is taken by the sheer beauty of the farthest stretches of the dazzling, jewel-like waters of the Atlantic Ocean.

At this sight you turn your head to say, "Wow, look at that!" to the person next to you, and you . . . Haaa-Woooooosh!! Down! Woahhh! This issss SteeeeP! Juuuuurn!! Make this thiiing turrrr!! Ohhh My Gosssssssh!! How diiiid thissss thing *evvvverrr? Swoooooozzzzzsh!! Mooove ooooverrrr ssssome wooooould yaaa?! Ohhhhh nooooooo, anooooootherrrrrr tttturrrrrrnnnnn!! Yowwwwww!! Whoooose hat isss thissss?! Ha-Rooooshhh! Anotherrrr drop!! Look!! Anotherrrr dro . . . Ahhhhhhhhhh!! Ahhhhhhhhhhh!! Ahhhhhhhhhh!! Get off myyyyy leg!! You'rrre smassshin' myyyy leg!! Ahhhhhhhh!! Ahhhhhhhh!!*

All at once your head snaps forward. The railcar screeches to a painfully sudden stop; and, making certain your neck still functions, you cautiously glance up and to the right, where a whole new set of fools eagerly await your exit. This you eventually manage to do; and while newcomers flood the vacancies you and your railmates leave behind, you easily remember that not yet a single minute earlier you had sworn to your God — and to the gods of several other peoples as well — that you'd never ride any amusement named after a natural disaster again.

It therefore amazes you that you find yourself in a dead run to return to the line's end, talking excitedly to anyone you've never even met before about the best roller coaster on Earth — and what a ride it was!

I rode the Cyclone six times in all, and enjoyed dozens of other rides and various sideshow amusements as well, before I left the park shortly before sundown. My time spent there made for some of the best fun I've had in years. But I'd like to complete this short letter to you, Aunt, by telling of an equally exciting bit of entertainment I stumbled upon just outside the park's gates.

As you might expect to find outside the fences of any such park, there were groups of children here and there too financially unfortunate to get in. However, one group off and away to the side had something going on that caught my attention to the degree that I stood by, watching their game well after sundown. They played in the bright lights the park cast through the fencing, and their style of toy fascinated me as much as the Cyclone itself. Had they owned the money to do so, I'm sure they would have been gambling it away on each other's best efforts in the game. But as it was, they were betting with the next most valuable possession known; and by the time I began watching, one young lady had already won nearly every marble in the group. But don't misunderstand, marbles wasn't the game. Rather, it was a contrivance of mousetraps on wheels that held these children spellbound, and other oldsters like myself paused in wonder to watch the things scurry off beyond the lighted ground into the shadows.

One of the kids allowed me to inspect his cleverly built machine, and I unwittingly allowed it to snap me a good one! But then being careful, I held it up there in the light. The Cyclone roared in the background upon its massive complication of wood and steel, and suddenly I understood how such enormous feats of engineering like roller coasters are really accomplished. You start out small, and you just keep going!

It seemed that many of the unusual forces that make a coaster so much fun were being played out in a miniature way with these amazing mousetrap vehicles, and I'd like to somehow describe them in words. But I think this is as good a time as any to let my rough drawings fill in for me.

I will finish, though, by saying it was uplifting to see so many kids find a way to enjoy themselves using their wits; and I would certainly not be surprised to see more than one ingenious soul from that group grow up to create things even more amazing than a gravity-powered thrill ride!

I shall soon write again

Love always,
Harmon

Eeeek!
What's this?! Not a single trap left in the city?
And mouses are out in the streets running wild.
What's that?! All the traps have been purchased by children?
But Why? How could those be of use to a child?
Aha! Now I see what these youngsters are up to!
I almost can hear all those shriek little squeals,
when mice in this town find that kids have invented
a new way to catch them
with mousetraps on wheels!

Laura had inspired the first part to coincide with her students' study and construction of roller coasters. The mousetrap cars were being built by my kids. Both are great physics inquiries, and it was great fun to intertwine the two in what appears to have been a single evening of entertaining experiences for Harmon. As I've said, nothing cannot be included when you're the designer! I continue to be pleasantly surprised at the arrival of mail from teachers letting me know how much their kids are enjoying the story and participating along the way. But by far, the most significant letter I have ever received came not from a classroom teacher, but from a parent.

> Dear Mr. Brewer
>
> I just wanted to tell you that I apreciate what your letters have did for Steven at school. He has a very hard time at school and it has kept his attention were his regular school work has not. He talks about Harman and the letters all the time and now he wants to come back. Thank you for keeping his intrest going.
>
> Sincerly,
> Mrs. Wanda Adams
> (I am Stevens grandmother)

Whenever I think it's time for me to seriously consider a way to have Harmon die off, I read that letter. Talk about inclusion. As far as I'm concerned, the old guy can live to be 150!

CHAPTER 7

CONTACT!

For the most part, the classroom and school yard are sufficient for the vast majority of inquiries concerning Harmon's past. Windmills, quilts, rockets, roller coasters, radio shows, silent films, music, mapping, women's rights, raptors, and visiting drivers of antiquated machinery all can be explored in those settings. But without question, the most anticipated moment is the gathering of schools for the annual talent fairs.

A thematic curriculum that incorporates multiple intelligences needs a special day of celebration for its finale. A curriculum that includes the many intelligences through numerous and varied inquiries will be spread out over at least a fair amount of the school year. By bringing a number of those activities back together in a single event, you will create an experience that kids will remember for the rest of their lives.

If your curriculum is used in other classes or schools, it is best to include those other classes in the culminating event. This provides great opportunities for your students to communicate, to interact, and simply to witness how somebody else approached the activities that engaged them. My own students are proof of this. Every year they are amazed to see the myriad styles of quilts, rockets, and windmills that are brought to the fair by students from afar. In addition to these, the variety of well-rehearsed acts, and humorous, clever commercials that are performed by kids from different schools opens everyone's eyes to the fact that creativity is truly an infinite collection of possibilities.

For the first five years of the program, Harmon's day of celebration was held at Cedar Farm, which is an incredibly beautiful private residence hidden along the banks of the Ohio River. The farm's owners, Bill and Gayle Cook of Bloomington, Indiana, graciously permitted hundreds of students to enjoy the fair there; and the farm's caretakers, David and Joan Steen, made all of us feel more than welcome. The historic, pre-Civil War farm is immaculately restored and includes a spectacular mansion, bright-red barns, a one-room school house, several guest cabins, and even a 4,000-foot grass runway, which was perfect for the entrance of an old freelance newspaper reporter in his World War I biplane. While in the first few years, students were introduced to a motorcycle-pushing young Harmon as he appeared from the surrounding woods, the Cook's own pilots later stepped in to make his entrance far more spectacular.

Pilot Nathan Harbstreit and Harmon streak over the crowd just after a few young scientists launch their model rockets.

I'd always wanted to fly in the open cockpit of a biplane; and for three scarf-and-goggled years, the aviating father and son team of Robert and Nathan Harbstreit granted me — and hundreds of onlooking kids, teachers, and parents — an array of awesome aerial experiences.

Teachers brought classes to Cedar Farm from as far as 300 miles away, meaning that students — even though their teachers occupied them with Harmon inquiries along the way — had to get up very early in the morning and spent far too much time on buses. For this reason, teachers in different schools within particular regions of the state began to come together for their own culminating day of activities.

The southern schools now converge on yet another scenic farm, this time in Lanesville, Indiana. Schools in the center of the state began having a fair hosted by either Clear Creek Elementary or Templeton Elementary in Bloomington, and the northerners now enjoy their conclusion at Perry Hill Elementary in Fort Wayne.

There are other participating schools that hold celebrations on their own, usually because of the traveling distance to a fair location or because of corporation restraints on study trips. But such barricades have inspired those teachers to create their own special memories of the classroom journey. All of these gatherings represent major, extra efforts made by teachers and community members.

Cedar Farm was a spectacular place to hold our own fair. But eventually the need arose to move. The stars of fate shown brightly on our wandering, wrinkled soul; and the Lanesville farm has fit the story perfectly. Accented by sprawling, open fields, it is owned by Jerry and Lennie Reinhardt. By luck, a local flying club's grass airstrip directly adjoins Jerry's hay field! The farm originally belonged to Jerry's parents, John and Wanda Reinhardt, and 80-year-old Wanda still lives in the farm's original white clapboard house. It is in her yard that more than 400 students of all ages have congregated for the past two years, and she has given the event her blessings. She would have been a wonderful Aunt Victoria. It was, in fact, in the tiny community of Lanesville that I selected to have a fictional Aunt Victoria live some 80-odd years ago, with her nephew joining her there as a young boy after his parents died. The students are all well aware of this through Seth's pre-journey video introduction, making Lanesville a rather magical spot for his grandfather to make his appearance.

But what about the weather? For whatever reasons the Gods on Mount Education may have, Harmon's culminating Talent Fair days have been exquisitely pristine for the past seven years. At this writing, I prepare for year number eight with highest hopes that our luck will hold. But if not, plan B will suffice.

Indiana University Southeast has a large hall called the Hoosier Room, and it is there that everyone can enjoy the program indoors if it is necessary. Of course, Harmon's biplane entrance will be out. But, as usual, a good friend comes to the rescue; and Sam Hecht's 1950 Harley Davidson is always on standby.

It is Sam's antique motorcycle that I have used many times at the Perry Hill celebrations. I just put it in the back of my truck, strap it down, and head for Fort Wayne. Jim Dowling and crew always put me up for the night in a nearby hotel so I can get up early enough to spend a few hours on the makeup required to push me over the century mark. But I realized the first time I made the trip that I couldn't leave Sam's pride and joy outside. The only choice was to sleep with it, so I always ask for a ground-floor room with an outside entrance to the parking lot. I just push it inside and bolt the door. With the Harley standing in the middle of the room, the two of us rest a lot easier.

It is a great machine (reminding me of several I've personally owned) and is as close to the 'real' Sir Davi as I'll ever need. It's rickety, it smokes, it's loud, and it runs! Kids are spellbound when they see me coming from a distance on it; and when I top the last hill with metal and bones roaring and rattling, I can read their minds solely by their expressions: "My gosh, there he is!"

And so, we have traveled from the beginning to what must surely be approaching an old traveler's end. It is my sincerest hope that, somewhere between these two points, you have been encouraged to record and share that which you already know will enrich the lives of children.

The assistants you need await. They will arrive in droves to meet the opportunities you create for them to be included. And the young people you seek to activate will most certainly follow suit.

From the moment I knew I would be writing of Harmon's creation, I realized the greatest task would be its concluding thoughts. Perhaps, someday, I'll have a few. But for now, I need to get busy planning our next talent fair. Of course, by the time this book reaches publication, 22 May 2001 will be yet another successful memory. But as I write, it is an abnormally cold day in March, with much to align before the biplane pilot yells, "Contact!"

The day's agenda has remained much the same from one year to the next. Jerry Cook, a high school social studies teacher, long-time friend, and best man at my wedding, did an excellent job as show emcee for five years. Now Bob Walsh, another great friend and a boom-voiced high school math teacher, has taken on the role. If you visit the Reinhardt Farm in Lanesville on a particular day in May, you might experience the following:

It is roughly 9:00 in the morning as you pull into the long gravel driveway leading to Wanda Reinhardt's two-story house. Huge trees surround it, and a deep wood fills in behind. Even from a distance, you can tell that something special is brewing. Hay wagons pulled together and the peak of a tall, large tent reaching skyward behind them strikes you as unusual. The adults dressed in antiquated attire and moving about with apparently important tasks add to your curiosity. When you are sure that other people really are dressed in the manner you had been told, you pick up your own somewhat ridiculous hat, which you have kept out of sight, and stick it on your head.

You drive by a yellow school bus parked in front of the house and park in a group of nearby autos. Then you walk to the scene and discover that many of those whom you assumed were adults are, in reality, students. Everyone appears to know their place in the completion of the tasks at hand, and there is a barrage of cooperative shouting from all directions.

Tom Huckaby, a member of the barbershop quartet: "Where's the bag with the ice cream scoops and the bottle openers?"

Student: " We put it by the horse trough!"

Quartet member David Kaiser: "Speaking of the horse trough, are we going to need more ice? We've still got about two dozen cases of Cokes that need to go in."

Student: "Hey, here comes the ice cream truck!"

David: "Good. Buy me a Push-Up."

Same Student: "A what?"

Tom: "Forget it. Different generation!"

A Schwan's Ice Cream truck pulls in, and the white-capped driver hauls out four large drums of vanilla ice cream, enough for one scoop for each of the more than 450 students who will be arriving within the next 45 minutes. The ice cream is hustled away by four more students, who put it on tables under a long canopy, which is still being staked into place by a group of uniformed boy scouts. Their adult leader, also in full dress, is placing orange cones near the tent's many guide ropes, clearly marking their position for the safety of those who will be walking in the area. The day is young and the air temperature noticeably cool; but the rays of a brilliant sun have begun to streak above the canopy, and their source is steadily warming an amazingly blue sky.

With the rising sun on your right and the house 50 feet behind you, you settle onto one of the hundred or so hay bales that have been placed carefully in arching rows. The ground slopes gently downward in front of you, and the sweet-scented bales create a sweeping outdoor amphitheater, permitting perfect viewing of the stage from any spot.

A young girl, perhaps in the seventh or eighth grade, calls out, "*Lanesville Gazette!*"

She's wearing a slightly too long, cream-colored, lacy dress that brushes the ground; and the brim of her overly big, white hat is covered with a swirling mass of ribboned lace, accented with a single, bright-blue, artificial flower. With an old newspaper bag slung over one shoulder, she tilts to one side as she lugs the weight of her wares. "Get your *Gazette* here! Fifteen cents for the best paper in town! Get your *Gazette*!"

No one answers her, and she wearily plops down on the hay bale next to you. "These are heavy!" she says, and adds with a laugh, "And I'll be glad when they're gone!"

When you ask, she tells you that she's an eighth-grader from South Central Junior High School and that she was in Mrs. Eastridge's classroom two years ago. She took Harmon's journey in sixth grade, and now she's a helper for the fair. She loves it. Not only is she spending an exciting day with excellent company, but she's out of regular school for the day! "All of us got on the bus at school and got here about an hour ago. And ever since then, it's been crazy! I knew it would be work, but I never thought my arms could get so sore just moving a bunch of hay around! Somebody said that last night Mr. Brewer left a note tacked up on the stage for us to move 'em all up this hill some more, and now I guess everybody will be in the shade a little longer."

She's a very pleasant kid, and you suddenly realize just how much work could be achieved by having a whole bus load of her type on the job.

You look and see equally hard-working students all around you, setting up tables, running extension cords, placing speakers, and preparing rockets. Many students check and re-check to be certain their disposable cameras are ready. For these helpers, the sole task is to snap photographs of students and adults from the school to which they have been assigned. In this way, all teachers will receive a booklet of pictures that were taken of their own kids at the fair.

To one side of the stage, you see a small group of student photographers discussing angles and particular subjects. Their task is similar to the "classroom snappers," but their mission is to get photos of the adult assistants throughout the day and the events as they unravel on stage. Finally, you see that an older boy has already used up an entire roll of film. His assignment has been to record a variety of things, including the set-up procedures; and he drops the small disposable into a cardboard box beside the stage. Turning your way, he spots you and your young friend and calls out, "Aha!" He approaches, turns his floppy, 1920s era cap around backwards to clear his view, and pulls another camera from his pocket. You've scarcely met, yet you and your *Gazette* peddling friend put arms around each other, smile, and in a flash become the next candidates to appear on the front page of Harmon's website.

The girl hops up. Students in charge of dipping ice cream have located the dippers, and she's ready for one. "Would you like one? Everybody gets a free dip!"

"Sure!" you reply. She leaves her bag of newspapers behind and trots off. Helping yourself to one, you see that the front page highlights the story of the Reinhardt's and of their farm's place in the rich and interesting history of Lanesville. Below this, you see a photo of the Harrison County Hummingbirds in full swing, and the accompanying article highlights a foursome who sound spectacular, even with their amazingly short schedule of vocal practice.

On the large inner pages of the *Gazette*, you find the names and graphics of more than a dozen caring sponsors who have taken part in the day's creation; and the paper's back page is covered from top to bottom with a collage of action from fairs of years past, with the picture of Seth Bidwell notably larger and overlooking the scene of collected memories.

Your ice cream arrives, and you thank the young lady as you hand over 15 cents, becoming her first newspaper customer. "Good!" she exclaims. "One less ounce to haul around!" She heave-ho's the bag and waddles away, and your attention turns to a strange whining sound that you can't quite place.

Though you are uncertain of the sound's origin, it seems to be coming from somewhere near the woods, just beyond the ropes, which have been set in place to limit the wanderings of guests on this beautiful piece of private property. A finely dressed man, whom you remember from a photo in the *Gazette* as being a magician, is now on stage, checking microphones with the classic, "Testing. Testing!" For a moment you think that the noise must have been feedback from the equipment. It's therefore no wonder that you're a little stunned to turn and witness a stout young man in full bagpiper's dress come thrashing up and out of the woods with his oddest of instruments wailing at high pitch! Obviously, today's celebration is to be a display of varied and unusual talents.

His private warm-up session is complete, and he unlashes his pipes, placing them on the edge of the stage. You overhear him tell the magician that he was practicing in his front yard one day, when a man driving a pickup truck pulled into his driveway and rolled down the window to enjoy the music. "I never saw this guy before in my life," says the piper, "but after ten minutes of explaining all of this stuff about some old guy named Harmon and that there'd be a bunch of kids involved in it, I said, 'yeah, I'll do that'."

The magician nods with a knowing grin. You take it to mean that a lot of people have accepted the invitation to contribute to the success of this event.

A few students have begun to tap signs into the ground. Each sign bears the name of a school. You look at your watch. It's 9:35.

At this point, a member of the Hummingbirds approaches and hands you a schedule of events for today's program. (You're an exception. Schedules are not given out to fair-goers so as to keep certain events a secret.) The Hummingbird is Jim Kendall, principal of South Central Elementary School. Knowing something of fashion, you approvingly observe that Mr. Kendall's dark beard beneath his bright-white, barbershop-style (plastic) straw hat nicely coordinates with his equally bright-white shirt and (just as plastic) bow tie. Proudly, he draws your attention to the act that will be next to last: "Right there! Precisely 11:08. Don't miss us. Best act on the agenda! We've been tuning up for weeks!"

You scan the schedule of events and find an impressive gathering of acts. But the one person you expected to see on the agenda is missing, and you ask about it. "Where does this Harmon character fit into this?"

"Hard to say!" says Jim. "But keep an eye out." (He looks skyward) "Could be from any direction, at any time! Time to go to work. Enjoy the show!"

The "work" he refers to is supervising as buses begin rolling in one after the next. You notice that, while student helpers do the dipping of ice cream and the dispersing of Cokes and Hershey bars, there is an adult somewhere in the background overseeing each task. You realize this is a good idea. Any potential arguments between visiting "unknown students" and the selected student helpers will be quashed by the adults in charge, and the "air of quiet authority" in place with so many competent adults completely eliminates the potential of such flares from the beginning.

"This way, please!" You hear a high-schooler shouting this to new arrivals, directing them to file through a quick line to purchase a fair ticket. "Twenty-five cents, please!"

For only a quarter, students receive a ticket and get their hands stamped. "Hang on to your stubs, they're the only one's you'll get!" Presently, you see tickets being torn along two dotted lines to make the three sections available for use. One piece will get the owner an eight-ounce bottle of Coca-Cola, another will be redeemed for a Hershey's Bar, and the third will be turned in for a copy of the *Gazette*. As for the accumulation of cash in the form of quarters, you notice that still another responsible student has been appointed as the official "banker" and keeps track of the money in a cash box. Not all of the services today will be donated, and the cash collected for tickets will help cover some of those costs.

High school band members, who participated in Harmon's Letters in the early years, have taken the stage to perform turn of the century tunes. They help to keep things calm while students settle into their new surroundings. Open sections among the hay bales quickly disappear with the arrival of each new class, and many are dressed in old-fashioned clothes.

You take a few seconds to look around at the hundreds of students who surround you. You try to think of one word that might sum up this event. Finally, it comes to you, "Diversity."

Glancing one way, you see the faces of second-graders. The front row is taken by the special education class. In another spot, you see lots of fourth-, fifth-, and sixth-graders making good use of their ability to raise the most racket. Elsewhere there are visiting junior high and high school students.

And adults are everywhere, not only in obvious roles as teachers, but as principals and superintendents in support of those teachers. Dozens of interested onlookers, as well as crucial and caring assistants, stand in large horseshoe fashion along the sides and to the back.

The emcee motions all of you to be seated. Fourth-graders from Madison, Indiana, are seated near you; and two girls in what are probably mom-made bonnets are talking in loud whispers.

"Where's Harmon?" says one.

"I don't know," replies the other. "He must be around here somewhere. Maybe he's asleep. Old people sleep a lot."

You laugh to yourself.

Pulling the agenda Mr. Kendall gave you from your pocket, you scan it quickly and then glance skyward. Nothing but blue. You'd like to turn to the girls and say, "No, he's not sleeping! He's up there somewhere, on his way to this fair in his old biplane!"

But that would be telling. And for all you really know, that might not be the way things work out at all! Plan though we might, flexibility must remain the rule, particularly when dealing with curricular jig-saw puzzles that are so large.

You look at your watch. Ten o'clock. Show time!

Sitting on a bench some 30 miles away, I look at my watch. I remove my schedule from the buttoned pocket of my heavy leather coat and unfold it.

"The band should be finished, and Bob should be starting things off," I think to myself.

Checking the agenda and time and picturing the goings-on at the fair is something I'll do again and again until I come into view of the event itself.

The day began five hours ago when the alarm shattered what little sleep I'd managed to squeeze in since leaving the farm around midnight. At 6:00 a.m. I ran through the checklist one more time:

1. Work boots and heavy socks
2. White button-down shirt and long-sleeved undershirt
3. Suspenders
4. Blue jeans
5. Hair dryer and extension cord
6. Tall mirror from my daughter's door
7. Antique spectacles
8. My dad's floppy golf cap
9. Notepad and pencil
10. "Harmon Bidwell: Freelance Newspaper Reporter" business cards
11. Leather jacket
12. Winter gloves
13. Blues Harp Harmonica
14. Peppermint mints
15. Wallet with Kelly's check
16. My schedule
17. Dramamine

After checks and re-checks, it was time for a brief breakfast. I had to eat something, but previous experience has taught me that only the slightest amount of toast and tea would do. I enjoyed it while standing on the back deck, watching the sun slowly making its way into a beautifully clear morning. "Good job, Ken!" I said out loud. Ken Shultz is a leading local weatherman for WHAS television, and he once "did the weather" on our RBC News broadcast at school. Since then, I have bothered him a week in advance of every Harmon's culminating day in hopes that he could help me plan. His prediction as of two days ago was that we'd have perfect weather again. Yes! We could put off holding the fair indoors at Indiana University Southeast for yet another year.

I pulled into the parking lot at Clark County Airport at 7:15 and sat in my truck, practicing on my harmonica. I'd arrived a full hour before make-up expert, Kelly Yurko, was due to meet me; but there was no way I could take a chance on somehow missing her. The thought that she could have car trouble, an overnight illness, or some other unscheduled change of plans has often made me wonder what I would do in such a case.

But that possibility always reminds me that my role in this day is just a very small part of what students and teachers have experienced throughout the journey. Sure, it will be nice if they get to meet the old man, but any number of the clever folks who participate in this endeavor can come up with a good reason why he couldn't make it.

At 8:30, Kelly drove into the lot and parked next to me. I hadn't realized I was holding my breath, but I exhaled in relief. For the past five years, Kelly and I have been meeting at this same time, in this same place, for the same purpose. I first found her by simply calling Actors Theater in Louisville to discover who did the make-up tasks, particularly the person who created old people. They directed me to Kelly.

She lives in Cincinnati, more than 100 miles away. Her fee is $225.00. The cost may seem high; but considering her travel, talent, and the fact that it takes almost an hour and a half to apply the heated latex to my face, the price and the results are excellent. The airport officials kindly allow us to take over a spot in their snack room; and the mirror, hair dryer (now used as a face dryer) and Kelly's massive tackle box of professional make-up are laid out.

Throughout the process, incoming and outgoing pilots and passengers marvel at the metamorphosis taking place by the Coke machine. One section at a time, my face is stretched, held in place by either Kelly's fingers or my own, then brushed with liquid latex. With the hair dryer set on hot, the rubbery surface on my skin dries rapidly. Then, when the tension is released, my skin returns to normal; but the latex stuck to it piles up, adding around 50 years. The mounds of wrinkles, deep valleys, and realistic age spots don't itch unless I think about them; and for the rest of the day, there won't be time to do so.

Now it's 10:15. I swallow two Dramamine tablets. Kelly's been gone for about 20 minutes, and I check my schedule. Skimming through my own scribbled-in reminders, I locate the spot where Bob and crew should be at this point.

9:30: High School Brass band begins. Schools begin to arrive.

9:45: Opening announcements. Emcee, Bob Walsh.

10:05: The Star Spangled Banner. Mrs. Eastridge and Students (Launch the rockets approx. two seconds before the line, "and the rockets' red glare.")

10:10: First Student Act. Mt. Tabor Elementary School Dancers

10:15: Bagpiper. Chip Schwartz

"Chip is probably in the middle of 'Amazing Grace,' wowing the whole crowd," I think. "Everyone I talked to after I arrived last year said that the tune sounded awesome ringing through the open fields behind the stage. I would like to have been there!" But I would never deny that the role I get to play is great, even if I do miss all but the very end of the fair.

I concentrate so hard on the schedule that I don't see Denny Doyle touch down at the far end of the runway in his white biplane. He pulls his plane up to the fuel pumps and cuts the very loud engine. He hops out and we wave to each other. His quick exit from the cockpit reminds me of how slowly I've always been in settling myself down into the seat of one of these things, but I have a slight excuse.

As a passenger, I ride up front, and the top wing of the plane sits just above my head. In order to crawl into the front seat, you have to duck, twist sideways, and ease yourself in place all at the same time. But being up front has its advantages. The first such advantage is that you look like you're the one actually flying the plane! And the second, and probably more luxurious factor, is that you don't get quite as much icy wind blown on you as the pilot behind you does. Each of you has a small windshield; but for the most part, you're out in the open air.

The temperature is supposed to reach 70 degrees by noon, and I've already worked up a slight sweat sitting and waiting in my latex-covered face and my leather coat. But in a few minutes, the wind chill I'll experience will be in the upper 40s. Thus the winter gloves and the long underwear!

Denny assists me as I step on the designated area of the lower wing and pull myself aboard. The word "EXPERIMENTAL" emblazoned above the dashboard instruments in front of me is less a shock than it used to be, but I still laugh about it. All planes built by their owners bear such a mark, and Denny built this one. It's a beautiful, highly aerodynamic airplane; but it has far too many seat belts! Once you are finally seated, one belt comes from over your left shoulder. A matching belt comes from behind the right shoulder. Another pair stretch up from the floor on both sides to meet yet another that extends from between your knees. All five come together at chest level, where they are linked with a special "T" shaped clasp that bolts them firmly in place. Essentially, you ain't goin' nowhere.

I take off my dad's golf cap and shove it deep into a pocket. Denny hands me my flying helmet. It looks just as you would think a World War I pilot's helmet should. It is made of heavy leather lined with fur and with a leather strap for buttoning under the neck. The big difference is that it also contains a two-way radio that allows Denny and I to talk and hear each other above the extremely powerful engine, which sits a mere three feet in front of me beyond a thin firewall.

The time is now 10:40. I locate the pocket my schedule is in and retrieve it for another check. 10:25: Storyteller Lee Cable should be finished, and the students should be performing their old-time radio commercials. In about five minutes, Jeff Russ will start his magic act. By that time, we should be taking off.

Denny has settled in behind me, and almost immediately the engine roars to life. The propeller, which looks close enough in front of me to reach out and touch, violently blows back the momentary scent of fuel. We begin to taxi to the runway's end. My cockpit has all of the same controls as Denny's, and the stick between my knees moves back and forth in ghostlike fashion. Looking down, I can see Denny's feet on either side of me, reaching forward to control the pedals for the wings' ailerons.

I've been kindly reminded to keep my feet off the ones in front of me, and I have no difficulty in remembering to do so.

While still on the ground, the plane's nose tilts up sharply as the tail rides on its small wheel, making it impossible to see anything in front of us. Denny gives himself brief opportunities to see where we are going by swerving from left to right as we move into position. At long last, and yet suddenly, I find that we are sitting at the end of the runway, awaiting takeoff. The image of Barbara Pedersen, an inspiring leader of teachers across the nation, flashes through my mind.

"Fly with both wings," she reminds us.

Though I intend to quite literally do that very thing in a matter of seconds, I know that it is meant as a statement of encouragement. With one wing, we must soar as high as possible in our chosen occupation. And with the other wing, we find our balance in the precious time spent with our families.

Voices crackle through my headphones. "One Clark County. This is Experimental 719DD ready for takeoff on 18."

"Roger, Experimental 719DD. You are go for takeoff on 18."

Denny's headset has a special switch. Placed in one position, he talks to people in airport towers. In the other mode, he can talk to me, and I to him. He switches to my mode. The engine grows even louder and vibrates the whole plane, and the propeller noticeably picks up speed.

"You ready?" he shouts.

Without hesitation, I shout even louder, "Absolutely!"

The plane makes a quick turn onto the runway, and the engine screams. We don't have to swerve to see forward anymore. The tail has lifted off the ground, giving both of us a full view of what lies ahead. In another instant, we're up; and I watch the airport and its surrounding mayhem steadily float backward.

Strapped in as securely as I am, movement is extremely limited. It is difficult to remove the spectacles from my nose and replace them with my real glasses from my coat pocket, but the view is well worth it. We have an extra few moments of time to simply enjoy flying before our scheduled landing, and flying is what Denny Doyle loves to do.

"You gonna' want to do some loops today, Harmon?"

I push the 'talk' button on my headset and answer in the hollow, 102-year-old voice I use when in character. "That will be fine with me, whipper-snapper!"

"We'll hang around up here on the outskirts for a while so they won't notice us. Just let me know when you want to get in close."

It's now 11:05. Jeff Russ' performance is about a half-hour in length. Jeff knows we're supposed to make our first low pass just as he finishes his final trick, leaving Bob to grab the microphone with a "Holy cow! What was that?!"

For the past few minutes, I've been trying to spot the school buses in the heavily wooded areas below. I know that Denny knows precisely where we're going — he's a member of the small private aeroclub that owns the grass airstrip — but still, I've begun to grow nervous about not finding it in time. Absolutely every hilltop, valley, road, car, and cow look identical to me. Realizing that we have only a few moments left, I reach to my headset and push the button.

"Uhhhh, do you see them anywhere?"

"Sure!" comes the too-calm reply. "We just passed the whole thing. Look to your left and back aways, and you'll see a bunch of buses lined up down there."

I wrestle with the belts to turn and look. Sure enough, I get my first glimpse of this year's celebration.

It's a beautiful sight. Hundreds of kids and adults create a multi-colored, living quilt laid out before a hay wagon stage. I can clearly make out Mr. Magic, still hard at work on the stage.

"I think it's time, Denny."

Without an answer, Denny stands his plane on it's head with an incredibly sharp turn and subsequent dive. We are on the scene almost immediately. Telling me to "Hang on!" he pulls the stick back hard, sending the nose straight up into what must surely be the lower realm of the ionosphere. My weight instantly triples, and I sink like a ton of bricks into my seat.

My lungs feel as though they are being squeezed through the spaces in the backside of my rib cage, thus explaining my inability to scream. I conclude that this airplane has far too few seat belts. For what seems like forever, the sky before me is rotating in some unnatural direction. Then, just as strangely, I suddenly see hills, a house, lots of people, and grown trees rapidly sprout from the Earth.

"How was that?" the aviator asks.

My sinuses, brain blood, and middle-ear fluids flood back into position sooner than expected; and I am surprised to find enough air left in one bronchi to exhale a wisp of an answer. "I'm sure they loved it!"

We land, and Denny taxis his plane within a few hundred feet of the stage. Like the Harbstreits before him, he has done a spectacular job. Later this morning, the kids will be thrilled to have their pictures taken with Harmon in front of a real biplane, making for one more tangible memory.

I take a final look at my watch as the propeller comes to a stop. This portion of the schedule was memorized long ago.

11:30: Special Guests Seth Bidwell and Friend on Stage

It doesn't matter what the schedule says at this point. Things are a bit unpredictable, and happen fast. As we climb from the plane, Ross Woodbury, the parent of one of my own students, drives his 1929 Hudson automobile over to us, and the pilot and I receive a brief, luxurious ride.

From the car's couch-sized back seat, I see kids ahead, stretching their necks with strained expressions, eager to get their first real look at Harmon.

Then, stepping from the car near the stage, I hear Bob's announcement. "It's Harmon Bidwell!"

Applause erupts. With so much to take in all at once, I realize that, once again, I haven't quite prepared myself for this moment.

Everything else seems to have been planned carefully. Yet, for some reason, I am again taken aback by the sudden closeness of so many unfamiliar faces.

Fortunately, my insecure reactions fit the script perfectly. I accept my arrival on the scene as the surprise it is intended to be, calling out, "Anybody seen Seth Bidwell around here?"

Seth immediately calls back from the stage, "Grandfather! We're glad you could make it!" And with the aid of two students, I slowly climb the steps. Once on stage, Seth and I hug each other. Bob immediately has his microphone leaning my way for comments. Taking out my pen and writing pad, I quickly make it clear that I've simply come to get a newspaper story.

"My grandson told me there'd be a talent fair here today, and I happen to love 'em! I'm just an old freelance reporter, looking for people to interview," I say. Seth steps in to assure me that I'll get my story. "As a matter of fact," he says, "I've already lined up a few candidates for that story, and they'll be up here in a minute. But first I have a surprise for you, Grandfather Harmon! Do you remember a trip you took way back in 1916 on a motorcycle you called Sir Davi?"

"Of course I do. But what in the world would that old clunker have to do with anything?"

"Well, do you remember writing any letters to my Great, Great Aunt Victoria while you were away?"

"I sure do. And to tell you the truth, I've wondered every now and then whatever happened to all of 'em. But again, what's the point?"

"I have them," says Seth. "And to help you become the teacher you always wanted to be, I made copies of them for all of these fine young people here today, and for hundreds of others in many schools all over the state. Your journey has become the class-room, and these are your students!"

I am very grateful, but find it a bit difficult to speak at this point. However, a huge "What have you got to say about that, Harmon?!" comes from Bob, the emcee.

My slow reply is, "All I can say about that is, 'let's play a tune!' "

My harmonica comes out. Lee Cable is immediately out front with me, guitar in hand and ready to go; and we break into an old blues rocker. More than a few are stunned at the get up and go a character of my age can produce. But after an epic classroom adventure, it's all nearly over; and the energy to be released at such a time is immense.

The last note rings, and Seth is again at the microphone to bring up those he has selected for my brief interview. After all, that's what I've come for. However, while I get in the first few questions, there are always comebacks for me to field.

Harmon has some questions of his own for a third-grader, while Seth Willis and Jerry Cook look on.

The first child is a girl from the third grade. She's precious, and she gathers up her long dress and holds it slightly above the stage floor as she answers my usual questions about how she liked the letters and what were some of her favorite parts. She's quick to give answers indicating that she paid a lot of attention in class, and then she fires a determined query my way.

"Did you really write all of those letters?"

"I sure did," comes a laughing, quick reply.

Smiling and apparently highly satisfied, she turns and walks away to the crowd's appreciative applause.

That was easy enough, but the second student creates a different scenario. He's a boy of around 12. He steps up, pushes back his oversized flat cap, peers through 102 years of wrinkled latex, and looks straight into my 45-year-old eyes.

I have no doubt about his upcoming question. I've heard it before, and I have the right answer for this time and place.

"Are you really Harmon Bidwell?" he asks.

I glance upward to a pleasantly smiling Bob Walsh. I see Seth Willis beside him. I look beyond the boy to the hundreds waiting for my answer, and among them I see a collection of gifted teachers. Each is a highly responsible instructor who has involved his or her students in one of the most in-depth thematic adventures they will ever experience.

I return my gaze to the boy and reach out to shake his hand. My answer is raspy-voiced and stated simply. "All I can tell you, son, is this. If there ever was a Harmon Bidwell, then I am most certainly him!"

Cheers escort the boy from the stage, and the Harrison County Hummingbirds come up for the fair's closing melody. I thank everyone for such a lovely day and begin to walk away. But Seth calls out that I've forgotten to speak with his third, and final, choice from the crowd. I turn around . . . and it's you. The Hummingbirds step back from the mike, creating for us a semicircle, pinstriped background.

"Well now, what can you tell me about today's celebration?" I inquire, pen poised to notepad.

You smile and say, "I can tell you plenty. I've seen teachers and other adults join in with the spirit of the history your letters describe. I've seen the business community creatively involved. I've seen responsible student helpers working hard and enjoying it. And I've seen all of these youngsters taking part in something I think they'll not soon forget. So I believe the time has come."

"Time for what?" I ask.

"For the crazy curriculum idea I've had tucked away in my mind for years to come to life."

I reply, "Now that's real music to an old man's ears! Let's find a hay bale and let these gentlemen perform. You've got a story to tell, and I want to hear all about it!"

*　*　*

Sincerest thanks to the following wonderful contributors who have helped bring the magic of Harmon's journey to so many young people.

The cast of players: Lee Cable, Karen Cable, Jerry Cook, Bob Walsh, Irvin Goldstein, Mike Carter, David Kaiser, Kyle Brewer, Seth Willis, Tom Huckaby, Jim Kendall, Jeff Russ, Bill Chilton, Chip Schwartz, Frank Wilson, Hilda Meyer, and Susan Eastridge.

Special contributions were made by: Charles Moman, Jennifer Brewer, Andrea Miller, Kelly Yurko, Sam Hecht, Jane Anderson, Robert Harbstreit, Nathan Harbstreit, Denny Doyle, Rocky Rake, Ross Woodbury, Todd Gould, Bill and Gayle Cook, Bill Carner, Betty Stem, Eileen Willis, Bill and Diana Hankla, Edmund Green, Roger Harper, Mary Ferree, David and Joan Steen, Pete Schickel, Walter Carter, Macon Ray, Wanda Reinhardt, Jerry and Lennie Reinhardt, Christa McAuliffe, and Tim Bridges.

Local and national sponsors: Hershey's Foods, Estes Manufacturing, McDonalds, Planters Corporation, the Federal Highway Department, the Oakland Museum Photographic Archives, the University of Louisville Photographic Archives, Kaiser's Warehouse, Coca-Cola Bottlers of Louisville, Wal-Mart, Bennett and Bennett Insurance, Geckler's Pools and Spas, Gerdon's Auto, the South Central Elementary School PTO, NBD Bank, Peoples Trust Bank, Colgate Palmolive, Preston Arts, the *Corydon Democrat*, Boy Scout Troop #47, Henning's Photography, the Kroger Company, and Woodbine Manufacturing.

The teachers: Irvin Goldstein, Susan Gahan, Mike Kaiser, Maxwell Monts, Alan Roederer, Jerre Patterson, Teresa Shireman, Kelly Misheikis, Laura McDermott, Jane Stewart, Susan Frieberger, Darlinia Rickert, Anna Cameron, Julie McDill, Donna Brewster, Susan Eastridge, Mary Mathes, Diana Hankla, Donald Dewey, Nancy Leininger, Brett Windmiller, Jim Dowling, Larry Rusher, Tama Rickelman, Rose Stevens, Jean Groskreutz, Jeff Pennington, Rick Tate, Terry Pierce, Janette Cox, Jack Morris, Andrea Chapman, Mary Ryman, Gabe Garman, Bridgette Knepper, Dan Ginder, Earl Howell, Keri Sackett, Holly

Matney, Pat Lyon, Renee Rodenbeck, Julie Burns, Tami Williams, Trent Shelton, Beverly Sweeny, Jeannie Kerkfhof, Karin McLean, Neal Lang, Cheryl Garrison, Monte Eckart, Becky Captain, Dennis Watson, Henry Poteet, Carol Goulder, Terri Ragland, Christine Pendleton, Marcie Lawson, Dana Flynn, Scott Burch, Gayle Hutchens, Michelle Collins, Valerie Gliessman, Myra Hogan, Kimberly Martin, Jeanette Stolz, Susie Moman, Peggy Conaway, Renny Reiman, Diana Sowers, Dave Marshall, Linda Fergusson, Dariel Coutney, Alicia O'Roarke, Debbie Cattman, and Emily Hatton.

And, alas, I thank Linda Ray, David Brengle, and Ginny Coppedge — three who have never met, yet independently fueled the idea of this tale with inspiring encouragement from the very beginning.